The Scott, Foresman PROCOM Series

Series Editors

Roderick P. Hart
University of Texas at Austin

Ronald L. Applbaum
Pan American University

Titles in the PROCOM Series

BETTER WRITING FOR PROFESSIONALS
A Concise Guide
Carol Gelderman

BETWEEN YOU AND ME
The Professional's Guide to Interpersonal Communication
Robert Hopper
In consultation with Lillian Davis

COMMUNICATION STRATEGIES FOR TRIAL ATTORNEYS
K. Phillip Taylor
Raymond W. Buchanan
David U. Strawn

THE CORPORATE MANAGER'S GUIDE TO BETTER COMMUNICATION
W. Charles Redding
In consultation with Michael Z. Sincoff

GETTING THE JOB DONE
A Guide to Better Communication for Office Staff
Bonnie M. Johnson
In consultation with Geri Sherman

THE GUIDE TO BETTER COMMUNICATION IN GOVERNMENT SERVICE
Raymond L. Falcione
In consultation with James G. Dalton

THE MILITARY OFFICER'S GUIDE TO BETTER COMMUNICATION
L. Brooks Hill
In consultation with Major Michael Gallagher

THE NURSE'S GUIDE TO BETTER COMMUNICATION
Robert E. Carlson
In consultation with Margaret Kidwell Udin and Mary Carlson

THE PHYSICIAN'S GUIDE TO BETTER COMMUNICATION
Barbara F. Sharf
In consultation with Dr. Joseph A. Flaherty

THE POLICE OFFICER'S GUIDE TO BETTER COMMUNICATION
T. Richard Cheatham
Keith V. Erickson
In consultation with Frank Dyson

PROFESSIONALLY SPEAKING
A Concise Guide
Robert J. Doolittle
In consultation with Thomas Towers

For further information, write to

Professional Publishing Group
Scott, Foresman and Company
1900 East Lake Avenue
Glenview, IL 60025

Better Writing for Professionals

A Concise Guide

SERIES EDITORS

Roderick P. Hart
University of Texas at Austin

Ronald L. Applbaum
Pan American University

Better Writing for Professionals

A Concise Guide

Carol Gelderman, Ph.D.
University of New Orleans

Scott, Foresman and Company   Glenview, Illinois
Dallas, Texas   Oakland, New Jersey   Palo Alto, California
Tucker, Georgia   London

ACKNOWLEDGMENTS

(p. 15, 18) From "Money Market Fund Hot" by Carol Gelderman in GAMBIT, March 8, 1981. Copyright © 1981 by Gambit Publications, Inc. Reprinted by permission.   (p. 28) From "Will General Motors Believe in Harmony? Will General Electric Believe in Beauty?" by Adam Smith in NEW YORK MAGAZINE, June 15, 1970. Copyright © 1970 by George Goodman. Reprinted by permission of International Creative Management.   (p. 52) From "Medical Writing: Another Look" by Saul S. Radovsky in THE NEW ENGLAND JOURNAL OF MEDICINE, July 19, 1979, Vol. 301, No. 3. Reprinted by permission of The New England Journal of Medicine.   (p. 74) From "A Stock Market Junkie Confesses" by Carol Gelderman in GAMBIT, December 8, 1980. Copyright © 1980 by Gambit Publications, Inc. Reprinted by permission.   (p. 77) From "The Rhetoric of the 1980 Election" by Walker Gibson in LOUISIANA ENGLISH JOURNAL, Fall 1981. Reprinted by permission of the Louisiana English Journal and the author.

Library of Congress Cataloging in Publication Data

Gelderman, Carol W.
  Better writing for professionals.

  Includes bibliographical references and index.
  1. English language—Rhetoric.   2. English language—Business English.   3. Report writing.   I. Title.
PE1479.B87G44   1984   808'.066   83-16309
ISBN 0-673-15563-3

CONTENTS

CHAPTER 3

Informative Writing   *39*

CHAPTER 4

Style   *63*

CHAPTER 5

Usage   *83*

CHAPTER *6*

Editing   *99*

FOREWORD

This volume is part of a series entitled *ProCom* (Professional Communication), which has been created to bring the very latest thinking about human communication to the attention of working professionals. Busy professionals rarely have time for theoretical writings on communication oriented toward general readers, and the books in the ProCom series have been designed to provide the information they need. This volume and the others in the series focus on what communication scholars have learned recently that might prove useful to professionals, how certain principles of interaction can be applied in concrete situations, and what difference the latest thoughts about communication can make in the lives and careers of professionals.

Most professionals want to improve their communication skills in the context of their unique professional callings. They don't want pie-in-the-sky solutions divorced from the reality of their jobs. And, because they are professionals, they typically distrust uninformed advice offered by uninformed advisors, no matter how well intentioned the advice and the advisors might be.

The books in this series have been carefully adapted to the needs and special circumstances of modern professionals. For example, it becomes obvious that the skills needed by a nurse when communicating with the family of a terminally ill patient will differ markedly from those demanded of an attorney when coaxing crucial testimony out of a reluctant witness. Furthermore, analyzing the nurse's or attorney's experiences will hardly help an engineer explain a new bridge's stress fractures to state legislators, a military officer motivate a group of especially dispirited recruits, or a police officer calm a vicious domestic disturbance. All these situations require a special kind of professional with a special kind of professional training. It is ProCom's intention to supplement that training in the area of communication skills.

Each of the authors of the ProCom volumes has extensively taught, written about, and listened to professionals in his or her area. In addition, the books have profited from the services of area consultants—working professionals who have practical experience with the special kinds of communication problems that confront their co-workers. The authors and the area consultants have collaborated to provide solutions to these vexing problems.

We, the editors of the series, believe that ProCom will treat you well. We believe that you will find no theory-for-the-sake-of-theory here. We believe that you will find a sense of expertise. We believe that you will find the content of the ProCom volumes to be specific rather than general, concrete rather than abstract, applied rather than theoretical. We believe that you will find the examples interesting, the information appropriate, and the applications useful. We believe that you will find the ProCom volumes helpful whether you read them on your own or use them in a workshop. We know that ProCom has brought together the most informed authors and the best analysis and advice possible. We ask you to add your own professional goals and practical experiences so that your human communication holds all the warmth that makes it human and all the clarity that makes it communication.

Roderick P. Hart
University of Texas at Austin

Ronald L. Applbaum
Pan American University

PREFACE

Better Writing for Professionals: A Concise Guide is for those people who are interested in producing the kind of clear, functional English that will enable them to face any writing situation. Its plan is simple:

Chapter 1: *Preparing to write* (preparation is 90 percent of the writing effort);

Chapter 2: *Writing the article or speech* (a survey of the whole process of writing);

Chapter 3: *Composing reports, letters, and memos* (parts or products of the process of writing);

Chapter 4: *Style* (precision and tone);

Chapter 5: *Usage* (grammar, punctuation, and commonly confused words which plague most people);

Chapter 6: *Editing* (detection and correction of error).

In addition, two short Appendixes cover parts of speech and readability formulas.

Although written concisely, this book provides a complete guide for business and professional people for their use as a handy reference. It can also be used by leaders of writing seminars and workshops.

I wish to thank Gary Huffman, Roberta Smedja of the Center for Effective Communication, Michael H. Murray of Michael H. Murray & Associates, Pamela Boughton of the Bank of America, and Jean Thompson of The Southland Corporation for comprehensive reviews. Thanks to Roderick P. Hart and Ronald L. Applbaum for their helpful advice; and to JoAnn Johnson Corrigan for asking me to do this book.

Carol Gelderman

A Conversation About Writing

THE IMPORTANCE OF WRITING

Lee Iacocca, ex-president of the Ford Motor Company and present CEO of the Chrysler Corporation, once told an interviewer from *Esquire Magazine* that the advice which helped him most in his corporate career came from his first district manager. The manager used to tell the young Iacocca when he'd burst into the office with an idea, "Stop coming in here and selling me with your hands. Write it down! If you can't put it succinctly, you haven't thought it out." The injunction is still valid today. An Amoco supervisor in Wyoming tells his engineers, "I can't do anything with your engineering if you can't explain it to me. And I don't have time to fiddle around with your ideas unless you've worked them into shape."

The ability to write well is a highly valued professional asset. *Harvard Business Review* subscribers recently rated the ability to communicate as the prime requisite of a promotable executive and of all aspects of communication, the written form, *Review* readers agreed, was the most important and difficult. The truth of this poll was brought home to six middle management executives of a large corporation in Chicago in a dramatic way. The six, all attractive, smart men in their thirties, had been hand-picked by the company to participate in a special re-evaluation of managerial practices. What happened was this: The company, alarmed by its inability to hold onto the young people it put through its training program, called in an industrial psychologist to find out what was wrong. In analyzing the situation, the consultant discovered there was trouble at all levels of management. To pinpoint exactly why there was so much dissatisfaction, the consultant decided to train persons who had worked for the company for several years to interview fellow executives. He identified six "comers" in the corporation, moved them and their families to Chicago, and arranged for them to learn every aspect of running the giant company. Their training, which included sophisticated interviewing tactics, was easily the equivalent of an MBA. When it was all over, the six were sent into the field—they would interview every supervisor, manager, and executive in the company.

All went well until their first batch of reports landed on their mentor's desk. While his six gifted interviewers could write correct sentences and paragraphs, they were unable to organize coherently the mass of material they had collected. Frantically, he called the chairperson of a university English department in the area for help. An instructor spent a week giving the interviewers (by this time yanked out of the field and pulled back to the home office) a quick course in how to marshal information into understandable and focused accounts. In short, they learned how to organize. They had to; having already been identified as "bright, young men," they understood all too clearly that not to improve their writing was to forfeit a big future.

Good, clear writing is a must for every professional. A hospital administrator who urged his medical staff to "take an aggressively penetrating approach to the communicative divisions of the interfaces between institutions of medicine," was passed over for promotion because no one could understand his directives. A few years ago the chemical division of an oil company spent a great deal of money reinventing from scratch a pesticide one of its own researchers had fabricated five years before; he'd buried the news 25 pages deep in a hopelessly convoluted report.

Ambiguous prose can cause as much trouble as convoluted

language. An employee died and left "half the value of my residence" to his company to repay money he had borrowed during the last year of his life. But his residence was located on a 120-acre farm. Family members questioned whether the man's will referred to the house and not the land. To avoid confusion, the will should have specified if he intended to leave half the value of both the house and the land or just half the value of the house. Unfortunately, the litigation which followed upon his lawyer's imprecise wording wiped out nearly all the value of both house and land. Both the company and family paid a high price for ambiguity.

Poor writers cost their employers money and jeopardize their own chance for advancement. Worse, if they can't write at all, they might lose their jobs. Recently, *Nation's Business* printed a story about two honor graduates of a highly regarded graduate school of business. They were called into a vice-president's office at the company where they had been working since getting out of school a few months earlier. They were fired on the spot. Why? Neither could write understandable memos.

Even so simple a matter as poor punctuation can wreak havoc on the budget of a project and the career of the perpetrator. A single hyphen omitted by a supervisor at a government-run nuclear installation probably holds the cost record for punctuation error. The nuclear engineer ordered rods of radioactive material cut into "10 foot long lengths." He got what he asked for—10 pieces each a foot long instead of the 10-foot lengths required. The loss was so great it was classified; the supervisor was fired.

Not so serious certainly, but disappointing nonetheless, was the needless loss of a grant because a professor made a silly grammatical error. She wrote an excellent proposal, and would most likely have been one of the recipients of a no-strings-attached stipend to do research work during a summer. However, she eliminated herself from the running when she wrote, "These two projects have grown out of my dissertation which I will complete this summer," because her university did not fund dissertation research. As it turned out, the professor had finished her dissertation, but the misplaced modifier, "which I will complete this summer," indicated that this was not so, and cost her $5000. What she meant was—these two projects, which I will complete this summer, have grown out of my dissertation.

Writing inadequacies of any kind—inability to organize, convoluted prose, ambiguity, grammatical error—dissipate an individual's as well as an organization's resources. Small wonder that Robert Schrank, a Ford Foundation authority on careers, believes that success in writing is the best long-run predictor of overall success.

What About Your Writing?

IS YOUR WRITING ADVANCING YOUR CAREER OR HOLDING
  YOU BACK?
DO YOU SPEND A WHOLE DAY ON A REPORT YOU SUSPECT
  SHOULD TAKE AN HOUR?
DOES YOUR WRITING RAMBLE OR LOSE FOCUS?
DO YOU USE JARGON AND TECHNICAL TERMS TOO MUCH?
DOES YOUR WRITING REALLY CONVINCE YOUR READER
  OR PROMOTE UNDERSTANDING?
DO YOU ALWAYS IDENTIFY YOUR READER BEFORE YOU
  WRITE?
CAN YOU WRITE MEMOS WHICH ATTRACT THE RIGHT
  KIND OF ATTENTION?
DO YOU USE VIGOROUS VERBS AND KEEP ADJECTIVES TO
  A MINIMUM?
DO YOU AVOID TRITE ADVERBS LIKE *VERY, EXTREMELY,
  REALLY*?
DO YOU USE THE FEWEST AND SIMPLEST WORDS
  POSSIBLE?
IS YOUR WRITING EVER AMBIGUOUS, POMPOUS,
  EUPHEMISTIC, CONVOLUTED?

What This Book Will Do for You

The questions about your writing provide an indirect means of telling you what this book will do for you. More directly, this text will help you:

GET OVER WRITER'S BLOCK
ORGANIZE YOUR MATERIAL BEFORE WRITING YOUR FIRST
  DRAFT
GET YOUR READER'S ATTENTION AND KEEP IT
INFORM AND/OR PERSUADE BY USING CONCRETE
  EVIDENCE
USE TRANSITIONS EFFECTIVELY
MAKE YOUR WRITING SOUND NATURAL
BURY THE TENDENCY TO USE STIFF, STUFFY JARGON
RELY ON VERBS AND GET RID OF THE UNNECESSARY
  MODIFIERS
AVOID COMMON GRAMMATICAL ERRORS
RUTHLESSLY EDIT YOUR OWN WORK

WHY THE BOOK IS ORGANIZED AS IT IS

The book begins where you must begin—preparing to write. Preparation is the most important step in the writing process. A thorough preparation will make the actual writing task easy.

Most professionals write memos, reports, letters, and proposals frequently; articles and speeches rarely, if ever. Why then is Chapter 2 a guide to composing articles and speeches rather than a review of the more ordinary writing forms professionals are called upon to produce every day? It's a case of looking at the whole first; if you can write an article or speech, you can write anything, even a book. This is because article writing calls into play every aspect of the *process* of writing: identifying your reader, limiting your subject, stockpiling and categorizing your data, finding your organizing idea, using concrete details as evidence for this idea, and pulling everything together into a neat conclusion. Learn the *process* of writing, and you can make any product—article, speech, report, memo, proposal, or letter. In other words, the writing skills you gain in Chapters 1 and 2 are applicable anywhere and everywhere. It's really just common sense: you have to learn a skill before you can apply it. To place the more technical forms of writing like reports and memos before learning the process of writing is to put the cart before the horse. Therefore, the writing of reports, proposals, memos, and letters is covered in Chapter 3.

When you have mastered the process of writing and can apply it to any product, you are ready to look at style, Chapter 4, the tone you use and the precision with which you write. Grammar and punctuation in Chapter 5 are important, but are the least difficult skills to acquire, so they appear near the end of the book. Finally, applying all you've learned to your own finished work is editing, logically the last chapter in this book.

CHAPTER *1*

Preparing to Write

Henrik Ibsen, whom many call the "father of modern drama," said he spent three years preparing to write a play, but only three weeks writing it. The principle, that taking sufficient time for preparation makes writing easier, holds true for everyone. Rigorous preparation is 90 percent of the writing task. Time spent in preparation saves time when writing. Not only will careful planning lessen your labor, it will make what you write effective.

IDENTIFY YOUR READER

Novice writers have a tendency to think primarily of themselves and thus to write primarily for themselves, and this is the reason for most bad writing. Writers can't ignore their readers; they must find out who they are and what they want to know.

Identifying and understanding your readers is the first important step to good writing. Dr. Sheldon Hackney, a past president of Tulane University, showed that he understood his audience (in his case listeners instead of readers) when he delivered a speech to a local businessmen's luncheon club shortly after arriving in New Orleans. The time was the early 1970s; Nixon was still in the White House and the war in Vietnam wore on. Assuming, correctly, that his audience disapproved of the disruptions on college campuses, Hackney opened his address with a joke whose point was that accepting the presidency of a university at that time was foolhardy. His listeners could easily identify with that idea. Hackney went on from there, cleverly bringing his audience from where they were—angry and disgusted with college students, to where

7

Ask Yourself

Who are your readers?
What do your readers know?
What don't your readers know?
Why do your readers want to read what you write?
What do your readers want to know?
What do they intend to do with this knowledge?
What will your readers understand without explanation and without definition?
What information must you elaborate upon?
When can you use a specialized word and when can't you?
When must you define a specialized word that you can't avoid using?

he was—somewhat proud of their response to Nixon and the war in Vietnam. Most likely no one in that audience left Hackney's talk with a determination to aid and abet Tulane students in battering the university, but most likely each went home with some understanding of what the furor was all about.

Before Sheldon Hackney wrote his speech, he assumed certain characteristics about his listeners. The kind of readers or listeners that a skilled writer imagines will depend on the occasion and on the kind of piece he or she is writing. This book, for example, is aimed at a professional audience. It will not, therefore, cover certain kinds of writing inappropriate to this group—term papers, for example.

A good writer "adjusts" the information he or she imparts to the readers who will receive it. To illustrate: A financial writer elects to do an article on money market funds for *Institutional Investor*, a magazine read by financial analysts, underwriters, brokers, and fund managers. Understanding that this particular audience will already know quite a lot about money market funds, the writer wisely delves into the complexities of commercial paper, certificates of deposit, Eurodollars, and all other types of short-term securities that make up the portfolios of money market funds in order to interest these particular readers.

Suppose, however, this same author decides to write about the funds for her local newspaper. Its readers, she reasons, will want to know what money market funds are, how they can invest in them, how safe the funds are, how the funds compare with other savings vehicles, why they are so popular; in short, why her readers should understand this investment medium.

Sensitivity to what your readers want to learn is important. In the 1980s, as technology continues to accelerate, you will have to write about that technology in simple and direct terms, being careful to use the language of those to whom you are writing. In other words, ask yourself, are you writing as specialist to specialist, generalist to generalist, specialist to generalist, or generalist to specialist?

An old country joke illustrates what happens when writers fail to adapt their communication to specific audiences. A farmer had driven his team of mules to town and was late returning home. "What took so long?" his wife asked. "On the way back," he explained, "I picked up the parson and from then on the mules didn't understand a thing I said."

LIMIT YOUR SUBJECT

In most cases, the nature of your job will determine your subject. If you are an engineer working on a long-range project, you will probably be expected to write a progress report from time to time. But even with so specific a subject, you should take pains to limit it so that its size is manageable. The way to limit your subject is to articulate your purpose in writing about it. Unless you know exactly what you hope to accomplish by your report, you cannot possibly decide what information it should contain. You have already identified the needs of your reader in limiting your subject. These, coupled with your purpose, enable you to establish the limits of your subject: the depth and breadth with which you cover your subject. In other words, by stating your purpose and your readers' needs, you will know how much detail to use. Your progress report will not, for example, include a set of firm conclusions or ultimate recommendations since these belong in the final report.

Often, then, the reason for writing is to explain something—the progress you've made on a project, a process, a mechanism, a theory, or an experiment. Sometimes your job will be to persuade an audience of the value of an idea or the usefulness of a piece of equipment. Whether the reason for your writing is given as part of your assignment or not, *before you start to write*, always decide what the exact purpose of your report, memo, or speech is, and make sure that every paragraph, every sentence, every word, makes a clear contribution to that purpose.

Never hesitate to limit your subject area fearing that if you limit your material too severely you will experience difficulty achieving a respectable length. The truth of the matter is really the reverse. You will find it easier to write a coherent, full report or memo of any length if you limit the scope of your subject. With your scope limited, you can fill your report or article or whatever you are writing with concrete, specific facts and examples.

Most people choose to handle a topic in too broad a way. It's safer, they think, to write about cooking rather than about a more restricted subject like cooking for hypertensives. Claig Claiborne and Pierre Franey understand the benefits of narrowing the subject matter of their cookbooks; they have turned out best-seller after best-seller by doing just that. Their recent book, *Claig Claiborne's Gourmet Diet* (1980), for example, teaches people how to cook without salt and not miss it.

Consider the author who wrote about money market funds: how did she appropriately limit her subject? The newspaper readers, she assumed, knew little about the funds since they were just becoming popular. She would show why. The readers of the trade journal already possessed this information; they needed to know why one fund was better or safer than another. For these readers, the writer would focus on the composition of a fund's portfolio.

> Therefore,
> the needs of your readers
> plus
> your purpose in writing
> determines
> the scope of your subject.

STOCKPILE DATA

Start by brainstorming.

Brainstorming is a process in which you uncritically, without thought of organization, jot down every idea about a subject which pops into your head. The key to successful brainstorming is that you do not attempt to evaluate or organize your material at this stage. These processes come later.

Modified brainstorming is using material you have already gathered. Take all your research information—your interviews, your letters, your notecards, your questionnaires, your experimental data—and sit down at a table and write on a notepad a list of all the facts and ideas in your material. Also jot down any ideas that your research materials suggest to you.

Your data should include facts, ideas, significant details, apt quotations, parallels, and impressions, but principally *facts*, because readers like to be taught, and they invariably prefer the concrete to the abstract.

To generate data ask questions: Why?

What?

How?

When?

Where?

Some people like to write their data on index cards, one point to a card (5″ × 8″ are better than 3″ × 5″). It makes no difference how you record your data, only that you do record it. By writing under the guise of doing something else, that is, collecting data, you aren't so likely to sit and stare into space.

Brainstorming the Money Market Article for the Newspaper

What is a money market fund?

Years to double your money:

$$\frac{72}{\text{Current interest rate}}$$

Why do funds pay such high yields?

How to redeem

How funds work

No sales charge

William Donoghue's book on money market funds

No government insurance

How to invest in money market funds

How to judge safety of funds

Explosive growth

How funds value their assets

Advisory help

Certificate of deposit

Money fund watchers: the surveys

Comparing funds by yield, average maturity, type of securities

Investment Company Institute

Managing funds

Variations of money market funds

Money Market Report

Purpose of funds

Money market funds started in early '70s

Good for small investor

Brokers' funds

Rowe Price Prime Reserve stops taking money

Common stock mutual fund industry took 30 years to get 50 billion

Targets of criticism

In 1980 funds' assets doubled

Congressional inquiries

A place to put money between other investments

Washington regulators

Interest rates in high teens

Surprise investigations in 1979

Severe back office problems

A bank account with a floating rate

Legislative efforts to strangle industry

Can cash in any time

Imposing reserve requirements

Big plus for little guy: gives him yields big guy gets

Is flow of money hurting banks and savings and loans?

Funds do not have to comply with banking regulations

Make funds deposit noninterest bearing reserves with the Federal Reserve System

Week by week income in 1981

In February funds took in almost 10 billion

In first six weeks in 1981, took in 15.2 billion

How are funds sold?

Minimum investment

Check-cashing privileges

Bank will wire money for five dollars

Moving assets

Surge began in 1978

NOW Accounts

Growing faster than any other type of fund in history

Distortion of money supply figures

CATEGORIZE YOUR DATA

After you have gathered your information, you will want to put it into manageable form. You do this by grouping, that is, by placing related ideas together. If you recorded your data on index cards, divide the cards into piles, one pile for each group of items closely related to each other. If you are writing about the automobile, for example, you'd put all the items about mileage in one pile, all the items about safety in another, all the items about cost in still another, and so on. Then you would arrange your piles of items in a sequence. Which are most important and should be given first or saved for last? Which must you present before others in order to make the others understandable? The point is, you will need some kind of order when you write your report. The order could be chronological, spatial, or hierarchical, that is, going from weakest item to strongest or from least important to most important.

Now within each pile, do the same thing; arrange the items in logical, understandable order.

What do you do if you have not used index cards? Look at the list of data that was collected for the article on the money market funds. Try to identify each point as belonging to a larger group or category.

Possible Categories	**Data**
Advantages	Why do funds pay such high yields?
How to invest	How to redeem
How funds work	How funds work
Advantages	No sales charge

How to invest	William Donoghue's book on money market funds
Definition of money market funds	What is a money market fund?
Advantages	Years to double your money:

$$\frac{72}{\text{Current Interest Rate}}$$

Explosive growth	No government insurance
How to invest	How to invest in money market funds
Comparison shopping	How to judge safety of funds
Explosive growth	Explosive growth
Comparison shopping	How funds value their assets
How to invest	Advisory help
Advantages	Certificates of deposit
How to invest	Money fund watchers: the surveys
Comparison shopping	Comparing funds by yield, average maturity, type of securities
How to invest	Investment Company Institute
Comparison shopping	Managing funds
Comparison shopping	Variations of money market funds
How to invest	Money market report
Advantages	Purpose of funds
Advantages	Money market funds started in early 1970s
Advantages	Good for small investor
Explosive growth	Brokers' funds
Explosive growth	Rowe Price Prime Reserve stops taking money
How to invest	How are funds sold?
How to invest	Minimum investment
Advantages	Check cashing privileges
How to invest	Bank will wire money for $5.00
Advantages	Moving assets
Explosive growth	Surge began in 1978
Advantages	NOW Accounts
Explosive growth	Growing faster than any other type of fund in history
Explosive growth	Distortion of money supply figures
Explosive growth	Common stock mutual fund industry took 30 years to get 50 billion
Explosive growth	Targets of criticism

Explosive growth	In 1980 funds' assets doubled
Explosive growth	Congressional inquiries
Advantages	A place to put money between other investments
Explosive growth	Washington regulators
Advantages	Interest rates in high teens
Explosive growth	Surprise investigations in 1979
Explosive growth	Severe back-office problems
Advantages	A bank account with a floating rate
Explosive growth	Legislative efforts to strangle industry
Advantages	Can cash in any time
Explosive growth	Imposing reserve requirements
Advantages	Big plus for little guy: gives him big yields big guy gets
Explosive growth	Is flow of money hurting banks and savings and loans?
Explosive growth	Funds do not have to comply with banking regulations
Explosive growth	Make funds deposit noninterest bearing reserves with the Federal Reserve System
Explosive growth	Week by week income in 1981
Explosive growth	In February funds took in almost 10 billion
Explosive growth	In first six weeks in 1981, funds took in 15.2 billion

The 54 items of information can be grouped into six categories:

1. Advantages
2. How to invest
3. How the funds work
4. Definition of money market funds
5. Explosive growth
6. Comparison shopping

The next step is to arrange the categories in logical order. It makes sense to start by saying what the money market funds are; next, to explain how they work; third, to detail their advantages as investments; fourth, to show how these advantages have resulted in explosive growth; and finally, now that the writer has piqued her readers' interest, to tell them how they can buy into these funds. Thus:

1. Definition of money market funds
2. How they work
3. Advantages
4. Explosive growth
5. How to invest

Notice that the writer left out the items identified as "comparison shopping." Because she did not want to get bogged down by the make-up of various money-fund portfolios (this material is more suited to the professional audience which reads journals like *Institutional Investor*), but because she wanted readers to know that differences did exist between the funds, she opted to bracket this information in a box. The boxed information serves another useful purpose: graphics of any sort break up solid text and give the reader a pleasant respite.

What to Look For

Yield
The interest the fund pays. A good fund manager can consistently deliver a top yield. Rowe Price Prime Reserve is an example of a fund having a top rate consistently.

Average maturity
Interest rates rise and fall. If you expect rates to decline, it's best to hold longer maturing investments. On the other hand, you will lose more with long maturities if interest rates rise. Short-term maturities are usually best. The average maturity of all money market funds today is 46 days.

Portfolio
U.S. government obligations are riskless, but the rate of return is lower than on other money market investments. Commercial paper, certificates of deposit, and bankers' acceptances carry some risk. They are as good as the companies and banks which issue the paper. Eurodollars which generally have the highest rate, also carry the greatest risk.[1]

Every good writer develops his or her own method of categorizing. For example, John McPhee, staff writer at the *New Yorker* and author of fourteen nonfiction books, has worked out a system that can help less prolific writers become proficient organizers. All of his work begins with extensive interviewing in the field. When he returns home he types up his notes (he does not use a tape recorder), adding other details or current thoughts. When he's finished he usually has about 100 pages of notes. He makes a photocopy and then reads and rereads them looking for areas he must flesh out with research and reading. This produces more notes which he types up to add pages to the original 100. He reads everything and makes notes on possible structures, describing patterns his writing might assume. Next he codes his notes using titles. These are his topics which he next writes on a series of index cards. After assembling a stack, he spreads them out on a table and begins to study the possibilities of order. A story has many possible sequences. When he has the cards in an arrangement that satisfies him, he thumbtacks them to a large bulletin board.

Now McPhee takes the duplicate set of notes and scissors its sheets apart, cutting large blocks of paragraphs and two- or three-line ribbons. The sheets become thousands of scraps which he sorts into file folders, one folder for each topic card on the bulletin board. These folders constitute an outline which McPhee files. Now he's ready to write.

He starts with the first index card on the board, opens its topic folder, further sorts scraps and ribbons until the segment also has a logical order. Then he begins to write his first draft. When he finishes a folder, he moves on to the next card, gets its topic folder, sorts it out, and continues to write.

This brings order out of the chaos of his notes. He's free to work on a given part of his work at a particular time. The other sections can't come crowding in to clutter his desk and mind.

John McPhee is a craftsman; he understands his work must have form. When you devise a system to structure your writing, your work will also have form.

FIND YOUR ORGANIZING IDEA

Finding your organizing idea is the most important step because it will determine the direction (organization) of the report, article, speech, or whatever you are writing.

How do you find your organizing idea? You might begin by re-examining your purpose. Usually, you will have had a purpose in mind while you were researching, but maybe your research has modified it to some degree. At this point write it out in precise terms. Nothing clarifies fuzzy thought as quickly as having to express it on paper. State your purpose with your audience in mind. Let's say, for example, that you have just purchased a Radio Shack franchise across the street from a high school. You want to let the students know how inexpensively they can buy an unassembled stereo. You decide to write a brochure outlining how easy it is to assemble the set. You will not merely write "how to build a hi-fi set," but rather "how to build a hi-fi set if you are a high school student with a limited knowledge of electronics."

After you have clearly stated your purpose, examine the results of your brainstorming. You are now about to bring order out of the hodgepodge before you. What you are looking for is an organizing idea—a one-sentence summary of the main idea to be dealt with in the paper. Such an organizing idea not only summarizes what the paper is about, but it shows the restriction of the topic. For instance, the organizing statement, "factory injuries could be alleviated by a better orientation period," limits the writer to dealing with injuries which can be related to a lack of orientation. Switching to a long discussion of at-home injuries or to injuries that are the result of drug addiction would not be relevant given the restrictions of this organizing idea.

The main function of the organizing idea is to designate your subject and to provide you with a rudder for maintaining its restriction and focus; with it you steer clear of disorganized writing. An organizing idea's name is its function: it organizes your data for you. Once you have an organizing idea, you know how to use your data—as evidence for your main idea.

The organizing idea should be a simple, declarative sentence stating only the main idea of the report, article, or paper. Avoid complex sentences full of subordinate ideas. If your organizing idea is something like, "In spite of the danger that many guilty parties may go unpunished by law because the resulting publicity may make a fair trial impossible, the Senate is justified in holding public hearings on wrongdoings in government," you've made life difficult for yourself. Your organizing idea should be "the Senate is justified in holding public hearings on wrongdoings in government." The problem with all the subordinate material in the sentence in which your organizing idea appears as the main clause is that you'll be tempted into a long discussion of things like "many guilty parties go unpunished." Many writers fall into this trap. By the time you spend several paragraphs or pages on the subordinate material, you're worn out, so as an afterthought you'll sail quickly through the real subject in the last paragraph or so.

Your organizing idea should suggest both what you intend to do in the paper and your attitude toward your subject. It should be expressed in specific, concrete language. Most importantly, the organizing idea must be an assertion, not a description. (Remember: an assertion can only be expressed in a sentence since you cannot say something about anything without a verb.) For example, suppose you must write a position paper on the increasing crime rate. If you choose an organizing idea like, "Both liberals and conservatives have views about the increasing crime rate," you have merely described the obvious. The only thing you can do now is to make out a shopping list: you can itemize what views liberals hold and then match that list with the views conservatives have. Your organizing idea must be assertive like, "The courts are responsible for the increasing crime rate," because now you have something significant to talk about. To say that both liberals and conservatives have views about the increasing crime rate, or about anything else for that matter, is like writing that some days it rains and some days it doesn't. You have nowhere to go when your organizing idea merely describes the obvious.

The purpose of the newspaper article on money market funds that follows was to inform the public about what they are and why they are so popular. Accordingly, the organizing idea became:

"Money market funds are more popular than any other savings vehicle in history because they have more advantages than the others."

Now the writer is ready to write the first draft of her paper. She has found an organizing idea and has sequentially arranged the categories of data which will support or illustrate that organizing idea.

First Draft
of
"Money Market Fund Hot"[2]

Category 1:
Definition

What investment yields more than 16 percent, carries virtually no risk, and is available to anyone with as little as $1,000? You would have to be living under a rock not to know it's the money market fund, a mutual fund that puts its shareholders' cash into high quality, short-term investments.

Category 2:
How money market
fund works

When large corporations, banks, even the federal government need short-term cash, they borrow in what is called the money market, a collective name for transactions made by wealthy individuals and institutions that have large amounts of money to lend. Because the borrowers want a lot of money for a short time, and because they put up no security other than their good name, they have to pay very high interest. It's a terrific deal for the lender. Until the money market fund came along (the first in 1972), you would have needed at least $100,000 to be a private lender in the money market.

Category 3:
Advantages

A money market fund operates on a simple principle—pooling. It receives relatively small amounts of money from a large number of individuals and businesses, pools that money, and lends it in the money market. The interest earned is then passed along to the fund's investors (the shareholders) as dividends. The dividends buy additional shares in the fund. So shareholders get the advantage of earning money market interest.

And that's not the only plus. You get check writing privileges at no cost, and your money continues to earn 16.2 percent (the current money market fund rate)* until your check clears. By contrast, the new NOW (Negotiable Order of Withdrawal) checking accounts typically pay 5¼ percent interest and require a minimum balance of $1,500 or more. And compare the money market fund's instant accessibility to a savings certificate which ties up your money for months, even years. Early redemption can cost you as much as six month's interest. Worse, the best Certificates of Deposit (CDs) pay 2½ percent less interest than any money market fund. (Of course, when interest rates come down, the money market fund rates will drop too.)

Category 4:
Explosive Growth

For the average investor, the money market fund is the most beneficial development to come along in the history of financial markets. And millions of people have recognized this. The funds have been taking in money faster than Ponzi. The surge began in 1978 when money market fund assets more than doubled in one year to $11 billion.

While that grabbed the attention of the financial markets, it was only a prelude to 1979's unbelievable performance. As inflation grew to 13 percent, assets of money market funds soared to almost $50 billion. The mutual fund industry took thirty years to collect as much money for its stock and bond funds, yet the money market funds attracted this amount in less than two years. During 1980 their assets doubled again, and the first six weeks of 1981 brought in a whopping $15.2 billion.

My own favorite fund, Rowe Price Prime Reserve, just returned a check I mailed February 14 explaining that "the unprecedented net inflow of money during the past few weeks has brought the fund close to having issued all of the 200 million shares authorized under its Articles of Incorporation." The fund has scheduled a special shareholder meeting for March to approve an increase in authorized shares.

Success like this does not go unnoticed. Banks and savings institutions are screaming their heads off that the funds enjoy unfair competitive advantages because they don't have to comply with

---

* Written for March 8, 1981, paper.

banking regulations. They want the funds to give up check writing privileges and to be required to deposit noninterest-bearing reserves with the Federal Reserve System. Since there is no governmental agency guaranteeing a shareholder's money as there is with a bank or savings institution, the funds say they have no unfair advantage.

Even the economists are complaining. They worry that the overwhelming popularity of the funds may be skewing money supply figures and thereby frustrating Federal Reserve policy. These experts point out that much of the money now going into funds comes from checking and savings accounts where it is counted as part of the money supply. But money market funds are not reflected in the official Fed figures.

It should surprise no one that the funds' explosive growth sparked Congressional inquiries and fired the interest of the Washington regulators. In the fall of 1979 the Securities and Exchange Commission ordered a series of raidlike investigations of all money funds—no small undertaking since there are over a hundred. SEC investigators made unannounced visits to fund offices and began unlocking desks and inspecting records.

After completing its inquiry, including an analysis of how funds' securities were valued, the quality of holdings, and the accuracy of yield quotes, the agency concluded that there were no irregularities. When asked why such a search was conducted, the SEC claimed stockholder complaints. The charge was true to a point; shareholders had been grumbling about uninterrupted busy signals when they tried to call their funds for a quote or a redemption.

Success inevitably begets some inconvenience, but it inspires imitation, too. The brokerage companies have not sat by idly watching this phenomenal growth. The typical broker hates to see a client withdraw cash from an active account, of course. All too often, the money never returns.

Yet if the broker has any conscience at all and cannot recommend any particular equity position for a customer, he has to suggest a cash position. For that reason, over the past few years, many of the major brokerage firms have set up their own money market funds which, like their no load counterparts, charge no entry or exit fee, and where their brokers can put their clients' cash. The money earns interest while broker and client consider other investment opportunities.

Category 5:
How to invest

Brokerage firms that do not have their own funds often recommend other money market funds to their clients and assist them into getting into a fund. A shrewd broker tries to give the impression that without his help, joining a money fund is somehow impossible. But it is not at all necessary to go through a broker or any other agent to buy into the funds. A telephone call or letter will get you the necessary prospectus and appropriate forms. You can get into the fund by mailing in its application form with a check or you can ask your bank to wire your money (costs $5) after you have called the fund on its toll free number and obtained an account number.

This out of place: it belongs in Category 3, Advantages. In a subsequent draft it would be simple to take out this one paragraph and move it to p. 19 before the paragraph beginning "For the average investor."

Most people use money market funds to park money temporarily between stock, bond, commodity, or real estate commitments. But at current rates, it would take only four-and-a-half years to double your money. (Last Christmas the average fund was paying 19½ percent; at that rate it would only take three-and-a-half years.) Not bad for a riskless investment.

For a list of money market funds with addresses and phone numbers, write to Investment Company Institute, the Washington-based trade group for mutual funds. For the encyclopedia on money market funds, look for the new book by William Donoghue who just sold its paperback rights for $400,000. New York publishers seem to want to get on the money market fund bandwagon too.

Not bad, for a first draft. The second to last paragraph, beginning "Most people use money market funds to park money ..." is in the wrong place. Since being able to park money temporarily and getting paid enormous yields while doing it is certainly advantageous to an investor, these statements belong in the section containing other advantages of money market funds, a section which comes much earlier in the article.

The draft was easy to write simply because the writer spent time preparing to write it. It cannot be emphasized too strongly—follow the five pre-writing steps closely:

1. Identify your reader
2. Limit your subject
3. Stockpile data
4. Categorize your data
5. Find your organizing idea

You, too, will write an almost effortless first draft.

Notes

1. From "Money Market Fund Hot," by Carol Gelderman in GAMBIT, March 8, 1981, p. 10.
2. "Money Market Fund Hot," p. 10.

CHAPTER *2*

Persuasive Writing

Since categorizing creates order, I'm going to divide every conceivable type of writing that you will be called upon to produce into two classifications—persuasive writing, to be covered in this chapter, and informative writing, considered in Chapter 3. Of course this is too rigid. Persuasive writing, if it's any good, will inform; much of what I call informative writing, reports, for example, will aim to persuade. The categories definitely overlap.

WRITING THE ARTICLE OR SPEECH

The purpose of persuasive writing is to convince or persuade, to make the reader agree with the writer's opinion, to take some action, or both. If you write an article for in-house consumption or out-house publication, you have a specific reason for doing this, either to convert someone to your way of looking at something or doing something. Similarly, if you write a speech, you have something significant to say about a subject. This "something significant" is the organizing idea—your unique idea, feeling, or opinion about the subject. There is a clear distinction between a subject and an organizing idea. The subject is that part of your environment on which you are focusing your attention. It's what your high-school English teacher called your topic. Your task is to discover the range of your potential responses to this topic, then select the best, most interesting, most persuasive (see page 17).

The Organizing Idea

Finding your organizing idea is the most important step in the process of writing. If your article (or speech) falls apart, it is probably because it has no primary idea to hold it together. On the other hand, if your organizing idea is sufficiently clear, it will organize your material almost automatically. If you do not find an organizing idea, your article or speech will be a tour through the miscellaneous.

Topic: What U.S. pays OPEC 90 billion in 1981

Suppose for example, that you are a banker who has been asked to give a speech for a local Kiwanis Club. Your topic is what America pays OPEC. You will mention the 90 billion dollars we will send to OPEC countries during 1981. But $90 billion is somewhat of an abstraction, even if you do add that it represents almost 20 percent of the value of all stocks listed on the New York stock exchange. You will talk about what we pay OPEC as the biggest and most rapid *transfer of* wealth in the history of mankind. You'll say that we buy this oil we burn with dollars because the world trades in dollars. But, you'll add, the hundreds of billions of dollars circulating threatens our entire banking system, not to mention the value of an individual's savings account. Worse, there are simply not enough goods in this country for the OPEC nations to buy with the $90 billion they get this year—and every year hereafter.

One fifth of N.Y. stock exchange

Transfer of wealth

Eurodollars and the banking system

Not enough goods

You could go on and on with equally startling facts, but how are these statements all held together? They aren't. However, if you had started with, "We are issuing claim checks on our country for something that burns up in the atmosphere," as an organizing idea, then you could use your facts to support this idea. The Arabs could, for example, use the $90 billion they get from us to buy every company listed on the New York stock exchange—and in less than five years. What could/would we do about it? Is it happening now? Are Arabs using frontmen to buy stock now? This great transfer of wealth, you continue, is occurring without our doing a thing about it. Will it be long before we are a colony of Saudi Arabia? Is this really such a fantastic notion? What about the billions and billions (soon to be trillions) of Eurodollars (dollars which have left America) that no one much wants anymore but about which no one knows what to do. Will interest rates ever go down to the 5 percent or 6 percent level, or must they be left artificially high so that enough of

Organizing idea

Same facts as above

Will Arabs buy U.S. industry?

Will Eurodollar glut keep interest rates high?

the wandering dollars seek a refuge in American banks? Without this money, will the likes of Citibank, Chase Manhattan, and Bank of America be forced to foreclose when the massive loans to Third World countries (taken out to pay for a product which burns in the atmosphere) can't be paid off or even maintained? What will the Eurodollars that don't end up in banks buy? Farms? Houses? Downtown real estate? Stocks? Bonds? You could go on and on showing how we are issuing claim checks on our future.

Will Arabs buy U.S.?

You can see the value of the organizing idea. Without it, all you were doing was listing facts, and startling as they are, this is not the way to write an interesting speech nor even a coherent one. But when you've decided on a focus, you make your facts fit that focus, be evidence for it, illustrate it. It is only then that you have something significant to say about your subject.

Since the organizing idea is so important, let's look again at how you go about finding one. *An organizing idea is an assertion.*
For example:

> Studying for an MBA while holding down a full-time job is tough.

> Studying for an MBA while holding down a full-time job has taught me not to procrastinate.

The first sentence is not an organizing idea. To begin, there is no clear focus; which is tough—studying for an MBA or holding down a full-time job? The second sentence is clear and focused.

> I will discuss the company's move to the sunbelt.

> The company's move to the sunbelt irritates me because I need the intellectual stimulation that only New York can offer.

The first sentence only announces a topic; it offers no clue as to what point the writer wants to make about it. The second sentence is decisive.

> How does the energy crisis affect people?

> The energy crisis has forced people to cut down on driving.

The first sentence is a question which could lead anywhere. An organizing idea must be a statement, not a question. The second sentence is an assertion which must be proved.

> Agatha Christie's stories are popular. They appeal to many people.

> Agatha Christie's popularity demonstrates nostalgia for the simpler days of the past.

A writer who uses two sentences instead of one to state an organizing idea announces that he hasn't made up his mind about Agatha Christie. The vagueness of "are popular" and "appeal to many people" suggest the writer is uncertain about his ideas.

> Ronald Reagan was elected president in 1980.
>
> Ronald Reagan's election demonstrated tne electorate's fear of inflation.

The first sentence is a description, it is a statement of an obvious and undeniable fact. An obvious and undeniable fact can never be an organizing idea because it allows no room for judgment or interpretation. Remember: an organizing idea must be an assertion, not a decription.

Concrete Details as Evidence

Let's assume you have scrupulously gone through the pre-writing steps described in the preceding chapter and that you have located a strong, assertive organizing idea. What do you do next? You illustrate that idea with details, details, details. Your details are the items you have gathered during your pre-writing preparation. You've brooded about your subject; you've discussed it with informed individuals; you've read about it in books and periodicals; and you've listed the information you've gathered either on sheets of paper or on index cards. You will have organized these details by stacking index cards into subject piles, or by making a list and writing next to each item what larger group you judge it should fit into (like the financial writer), or by culling topics from your accumulated notes and filing information bits in folders corresponding to these topics (like John McPhee), or by any system you can devise that organizes.

The important point about these details that you will use as illustrations of your organizing idea is that they be concrete, not vague. Richard Mitchell, an English professor at Glassboro State College, employs a wonderful example to show how important specificity is in his entertaining book, *Less Than Words Can Say* (1980):

> Imagine that you are chatting with Marco Polo, just back from Cathay, and you're burning to hear all about those strange people in a distant land. You ask what wonderful things he saw there; he tells you "marvels." You ask what the people wear; he tells you "attire." What do they grow; "crops." And their processes; what are they made of? "Components." Now you know all about Cathay.[1]

Of course, you know nothing about Cathay. But people do use "details" like this and think they are illustrating their ideas. The following sketch is another example:

Sports have played a major role in my life. My interest in sports began when I was just a youngster. In the earlier part of my life, I played _____. Ever since then I had a great interest in sports whether it was participating or just being a spectator.

Through high school, I participated in intramural sports as well as being on the _____ team. I find that by playing _____ you can relax and free yourself for a while from the problems of everyday life. Although at times you can feel pressure and tension, this happens only during tournament play. While playing in a tournament if you lose you have to face the agony of defeat. But, if you are victorious there is the ecstasy of winning.

In _____, like other sports, there is much disappointment. When you become better at the game there is a great sense of accomplishment. For these reasons, I place sports high on my list of priorities. I would participate or be a spectator in a sporting event before I would do a lot of other things.

I continued my interest in sports in college and graduate school. I played on my class _____ team as an undergraduate and took up _____ when a graduate student. Even now, ten years out of school, I play _____ and _____ every weekend.

Being active in sports is a good way to stay in good physical shape. After you have had a good workout you will feel better mentally as well as physically.

I needn't tell you that this "paper" lacks concrete details. Each mention of a specific sport was deleted to show you that a reader has no idea which sport or sports are being talked about without explicit nomenclature. In this instance, the writer was speaking of tennis and racquet ball. Had he written well, his readers would have known what sports he extolled even without their being named, by the specificity of details, details characteristic of tennis and racquet ball.

Read the following description, one loaded with concrete details, and see if you can tell what sport is pictured.

It has been customary to refer to _____ as shuffleboard on ice. In _____ the players zip a huge stone along the ice, the game getting its name from the peculiar twist—or _____—which experts are able to get into the speeding stone. The stones weigh 44 pounds and are 36 inches in circumference and 4½ inches in height.

_____ is played on ice, usually in an indoor rink 42 yards in length. Each team is made up of four men. Each player _____ two stones alternately with his opponent. The player swings the stone back, clear of the ice much in the same manner as one who is delivering a bowling ball and skims the surface of the ice with a smooth follow-through. At the instant he releases the stone, the player gives the handle either an in-turn or an out-turn, which is accomplished by a twist of the wrist that gives the stone a one-quarter turn and imparts to it the _____ action, which is nothing more nor less than a long curve.

The skip, or captain, always figures out the plays and designates with his broom where he wants the stone laid which is being played by his team member.

After all sixteen stones have been played, that end is completed and the score for that end is counted. The scoring side receives one point for each stone inside the "House," the "House" being the designation given to the target. The customary game consists of ten or twelve ends.

Anyone who has ever attended a curling match will recognize an exact depiction of the old Scottish sport. But even if you have never heard of curling, you can imagine the way the sport is played by this clear-cut, no-nonsense decription.

Let's look at another paragraph, this by an educator, which lacks the specificity of the curling explication, and see what can be done to change it from the abstract to the concrete.

Discipline is the most important factor for a teaching situation. Without it much learning, desired learning, cannot take place effectively. But it must be recognized that too stern a disciplinary procedure could result in puppet responses. It is a difficult problem and any teacher who can control the pupils both physically and mentally is a superior individual.

What advice can we offer the educator who wrote the paragraph to "concretize" his passage?

Focus on a particular situation in which, thanks to a teacher's discipline, either you or someone you know of, learned something. (Where were you/he/she and when? What happened? What did the teacher do that you call discipline? What exactly did you/he/she learn?)

Focus on another particular situation in which, thanks to too stern a discipline, you/he/she found yourself/himself/herself making a puppet response. (Where were you/he/she and when? What happened? What did the teacher do that was "too stern"? Just what was your/his/her puppet response?)

In your experience, what is the difference between learning something and making a puppet response?

It is, you say, a "difficult problem," and no one could disagree. But just what is this "discipline" that is "the most important factor for a teaching situation"? What advice can you suggest for teachers who want to bring about "desired learning"?

Always beware of intangible words—nouns like *discipline, love, honor, patriotism,* and so on. These are big abstractions; they are "catch-basins" into which you can pour just about anything. If you are forced to use abstract nouns like these, define *exactly* what you mean by them.

Conclusion

You've almost finished your article or speech. You've made a positive predication which serves as your organizing idea; you've particularized it with evidence made up of myriad details; now all you need is a conclusion. An ideal conclusion will:

summarize or recapitulate your argument
allude back to your introduction
carry your organizing idea a step further

Sample Article and Speech

The following, both a speech and an article, embodies a nice beginning (organizing idea), middle (illustration of the idea by concrete examples), and end (conclusions with three parts). It was written in 1970.

Introduction. A powerful lead or introduction can make or break a piece of writing. If an introduction doesn't hook the reader, he or she may not go further. The feature articles on the first page of *The Wall Street Journal* consistently illustrate imaginative ways of getting into an article. Study them.

A good introduction will also announce the organizing idea (the focus) of the speech or article. The organizing idea: underlined.

Why it will affect us all; details which illustrate this aspect of organizing idea.

John Hancock was a revolutionary, not a . . . life insurance salesman.*

Well, you might expect that as a bit of graffiti in Harvard Square. You get a lot of handwriting on the wall these days at our major universities, wall culture, just like Peking and Paris. The handwriting on the wall is anti, as you might expect. Nobody is going to write VIVA NIXON on a wall anywhere. And there is a certain amount of revolutionary chatter in the air. It is hard to take the revolutionary chatter seriously, because it always seems to have the cadence of 1882 Marxism, and the world does move on. . . .

There is, however, one glimmer of a . . . revolution, and if it is real, and continues, then it will affect all of us. To tell you about it I also have to tell you about a recent visit to Cambridge, because that is where the glimmer took place. Once a year for the past couple of years I have gone up to the Harvard Business School as a guest lecturer. No, the Business School is not exactly a hotbed of revolutionary activity. It likes to think of itself as the West Point of capitalism, and it certainly has provided one of the great Old Boy networks of modern times. Let a Business School type foul up out there in the world and he need not fear, another Business School type will come to his rescue and they will call it merger, or recapitalization, or synergy, or something. The ambitions of the Harvard Business School types are very simple. They want to run things. Why not, since the previous B-School generation already does? By "things" I mean everything; start with the great corporations of this country and continue to the government. . . . If there is some sort of revolution going on, these types will either lead it or fight it or try to take it over after it gets going.

* Ellipsis (. . .) indicates that words have been left out.

The two details which illustrate the glimmer of a revolution, the other part of the organizing idea.

I have two straws in the wind to submit:

A Class. The Guest Lecturer has posed a Case. You are running a portfolio of a hundred million dollars. . . . Company A is a notorious polluter, but its profits are unimpaired. Company B is buying anti-pollution equipment that will depress its profits for years. . . . You want to achieve performance in your portfolio, and this performance is being measured competitively. It may affect your career. Do you buy Company A, the profitable polluter, or Company B, the unprofitable anti-polluter?

Student One: "I would try to evaluate the long-term effect because in the long run Company B is going to have a better image."

Student Two: "But in the long run you would have lost the account. I think you have to know the wishes of the constituency. If it's a fund, how do the fund-holders feel? What do they want?" . . .

Student Three: "I buy the polluter. . . . It isn't the business of a fund manager to make a social decision, or to discriminate between companies on his own ideas of some social purpose. . . . You can't ask profit-making organizations to subsidize society."

The Radical Student: . . . "Maybe," says the Radical Student, "that's the problem. Everything in this school is geared to the purpose of the corporation, and that purpose is maximizing profit."

We ask the Radical Student: "What are the goals of corporations if not to maximize profit?"

Silence in the classroom, a rustling of papers. The idea is, after all, a bit confusing. . . .

You wouldn't have had this bit of dialogue three years ago.

My second item is The Resolution. . . .

These "two straws" provide concrete evidence for the writer's organizing idea.

The Business School voted and passed this, and then bought an ad in the *Wall Street Journal* to publicize it. The Resolution winds up calling for American withdrawal from Southeast Asia. . . . But now look at the language of the rest of the Resolution. It doesn't sound like the good old Republican, profit-maximizing Business School:

We condemn the administration of President Nixon . . . which:

1. Perceives the anxiety and turmoil in our midst as the work of "bums and effete snobs";
2. Fails to acknowledge that legitimate doubt exists about the ability of black Americans and other depressed groups to obtain justice;
3. Is unwilling to move for a transformation of American society in accordance with the goals of maximum fulfillment for each human being and harmony between mankind and nature.

[Harmony between mankind and nature?]*

I asked the former dean of admissions what was this about harmony between mankind and nature.

"I don't know," he said. "I guess it means they're not going to work for Procter and Gamble and make those dishwasher soaps that don't dissolve and smother the lakes. . . .

---

* Brackets [ ] indicate the author is making an editorial comment on the resolution; obviously his comment was not part of the resolution.

"If you asked the guys in the fifties," said the ex-dean, "the goal was to run the Big Company, and the guys in the sixties wanted to . . . make a nice bundle by the time you're 40 and then run for Congress and do something for the country."

"And now?"

"And now, they're just confused. I've never seen such malaise. . . ."

Why a glimmer and not a full-fledged revolution?

It is, of course, not a revolutionary idea in the history of this country to make something for less than a maximum profit. When the bulk of business was family-owned, its purpose was to take care of the family—sons, nephews, and so on—and of the product's reputation, if it had a reputation of value. So a wagonmaker could simply make a good wagon, and a book publisher could publish an author simply because he wanted to. What we have come to call social purpose was a matter of individual integrity, randomly and haphazardly applied.

But these businesses sold out to bigger ones, and those in turn to bigger ones. Multimillion-dollar businesses had to treasure objectivity and the quantification of results, and to manage those results on a massive scale we could no longer have intuition or seat-of-the-pants engineering. . . .

Conclusion. Allusion to the middle of the article which ties the whole thing together.

Maximum fulfillment for each human being? Harmony between man and nature? What kind of goals are these for the Harvard Business School? How are we going to put these things into a balance sheet? Can we operate a corporate society without objectivity? What is this, Zen Capitalism? . . .

Allusion to beginning of the article which helps to tie the whole together.

You can see why, if all of this is real and persists, that it is more revolutionary than the hard Left chanting, "Off the pigs." For if the Harvard Business School has moved from conservatism to confusion, that is a giant step. I am not sure the rhetoric will outlast the summer air, but if it does, well, our Lord Keynes did say, "I am sure that power of vested interests is vastly exaggerated compared with the gradual encroachment of ideas."

Taking main point a step further.

Will General Motors believe in the harmony between man and nature? Will General Electric believe in beauty and truth?

George Goodman, author of *The Money Game, Super Money,* and *Paper Money,* who writes under the name "Adam Smith," with quotation marks to emphasize that he is not the eighteenth-century economist, has written a first-rate speech/article. He introduces his subject, radical change, and then announces his organizing idea, "There is, however, one glimmer of a revolution, and if it is real, and continues, then it will affect all of us."

There are two parts to this organizing idea—what unusual change is occurring at the Harvard Business School and why this change will affect us all. He starts with the second part first; the change will affect us because the people who earn a Harvard MBA usually end up running the government and the big corporations of America, so what they think will affect what they do and what they do will affect all of us.

The first part of the organizing idea, that a "glimmer of a revolution" exists at Harvard is illustrated by two vivid details, the class discussion about portfolio management and the resolution the students publish in the *Wall Street Journal*. It's the concreteness of these details that makes this speech come alive. It's easy to picture a less gifted writer handling the same phenomenon, but using abstract terms, thereby making the piece boring.

Finally, Mr. Goodman executes a perfect conclusion. He summarizes the whole argument: "Maximum fulfillment for each human being? Harmony between man and nature? What kind of goals are these for the Harvard Business School? How are we going to put these things in a balance sheet? Can we operate a corporate society without objectivity? What is this, Zen Capitalism?"

He alludes back to the beginning: "And you can see why, if all this is real and persists, that it is more revolutionary than the hard Left chanting, 'Off the pigs' "; and he alludes to the middle: "Maximum fulfillment for each human being? Harmony between man and nature?"

Then he takes the whole argument a step further: "I am not sure the rhetoric will outlast the summer air, but if it does, well, our Lord Keynes did say, 'I am sure that power of vested interests is vastly exaggerated compared with the gradual encroachment of ideas.' But will the Fortune 500 soon accept these new ideas? Will General Motors believe in the harmony between man and nature? Will General Electric believe in beauty and truth?"

Coherence

Goodman's piece is successful because it provides a strong, assertive organizing idea, concrete illustrations of that idea, and a conclusion which ties everything neatly together. But there is more to be learned from Goodman. All good writing must have continuity. Never permit yourself to write a sentence that is not clearly connected to the ones immediately preceding and following it. The sequence must be self-evident. A reader should be able to see how each statement follows from statements that have come before it and leads to those that come after. A coherent paper reveals its own internal consistency by showing how the assertions are related. "2, 4, 6, 8, 10." You're aware of the coherence of this set. It readily reveals its principle of relationship. This set creates an expectation of an interval of 2 and then fulfills that expectation. "2, 4, 6, 3, 14." This set is not coherent because its sequential logic is not self-evident. The set establishes an expected interval between numbers and then contradicts that interval. It fails to reveal a principle of relationship. It is, therfore, incoherent. So, too, with writing. To develop a coherent paper, the writer must reveal the sequential logic of a system of statements, a line of reasoning. If the paper reveals no sequential logic, it is incoherent. Continuity ensures coherence. If you have a clear understanding of what you want to say, and if you occasionally repeat key words to make smooth transitions from sentence to sentence and from paragraph to paragraph, you'll end up with a strong continuity of argument. Look at the first few sentences of Goodman's article.

> "John Hancock was a revolutionary, not an obscene insurance salesman."
>
> Well, you might expect *that* as a bit of graffiti in Harvard Square. You get a lot of *handwriting on the wall* these days at our major universities, wall culture, just like Peking and Paris. *The handwriting on the wall* is anti, as you might expect. Nobody is going to write *Viva Nixon* on a *wall* anywhere. And there is a certain amount of *revolutionary chatter* in the air. It is hard to take the *revolutionary chatter* seriously, because it always seems to have the cadence of 1882 Marxism, and the world does move on.[3]

The first paragraph is a sample of graffiti seen in Harvard Square. The transition into the second paragraph is the word "that" which refers to "John Hancock was a revolutionary," which is the graffiti. "Handwriting on the wall," in the second sentence of the second paragraph, is what graffiti is. The third sentence repeats, "handwriting on the wall," and calls it "anti." The "Viva Nixon" in the fourth sentence is pro-sentiment which no one would write on a wall, picking up on "handwriting on the wall." "Revolutionary chatter," introduced by "and" in the fifth sentence is what the graffiti in Harvard Square is—"revolutionary chatter," and nothing else. The sixth sentence repeats "revolutionary chatter." The point is—continuity doesn't happen by itself; you've got to make it happen just as George Goodman did. Each sentence must be connected to the ones immediately preceding and following; carefully use pronouns *this* and *that*; keep a list of handy connectives like:

above all	in addition	moreover
accordingly	in conclusion	nevertheless
besides	in fact	similarly
consequently	in particular	therefore
for example	instead	yet
furthermore		

Another device for providing continuity is to use numbers or letters such as:

first, second, third
one, another, still another
(1), (2), (3)
(a), (b), (c)
first, next, finally

But there's more to continuity than using linking words. Every good article or speech will have a clear plan of attack, or, to put it another way, strong continuity of argument. Without this your writing will lack coherence.

The basic aim of coherence is to help your reader see how you are making connections between ideas. Problems in coherence often stem from the fact that you know your subject so well that the connection between its main points seems perfectly clear, perhaps even obvious. But readers don't know your subject in the same way you do, so you've got to make the relationships between points very carefully.

Your organizing idea announces your plan—your main point in your paper. However, this alone will not guarantee coherence. What if later in the body of the paper you don't follow the previously announced plan? Not only are your readers lost; so are you. Or what if your paper is complicated? Your readers may have trouble remembering your organizing idea. It's your job to remind them periodically of your overall focus. This also forces you to stick to your subject and prevents you from introducing nonrelevant material.

Your categories are your topics which illustrate your overall focus. Topic statements are to your paragraphs what the organizing idea is to the entire paper: they announce what will be covered in a paragraph. After you've written anything, a way to check its coherence is to underline its organizing idea and then the topic sentence from each subsequent paragraph. Do these together provide an outline of your paper's construction? Is this outline logical? If so, your paper is coherent.

As you become more comfortable as a writer, you might want to try other strategies of coherence. Instead of viewing the opening sentence of each paragraph as a topic sentence, try this idea from John Trimble (*Writing with Style*, 1975): View it as a *"bridge sentence"* whose prime function is to convey the reader over into the new paragraph.

Below are a number of paragraph openers from an oft-repeated article by Bergen Evans called, "But What's a Dictionary For?" (first published in *The Atlantic Monthly*, May 1962). They will illustrate the bridging technique graphically:[4]

> a. What underlines all this sound and fury?
>
> b. So monstrous a descrepancy in evaluation requires us to examine basic principles.
>
> c. Yet wild wails arose.
>
> d. More subtly, but persuasively, it has changed under the influence of mass education and the growth of democracy.
>
> e. And the papers have no choice.
>
> f. And so back to our questions: What's a dictionary for, and how, in 1962, can it best do what it ought to do?
>
> g. Even in so settled a matter as spelling, a dictionary cannot always be absolute.
>
> h. Has he been betrayed?
>
> i. Under these circumstances, what is a dictionary to do?
>
> j. An illustration is furnished by an editorial in the Washington *Post* (January 17, 1962).
>
> k. In part, the trouble is due to the fact that there is no standard for standard.

Even out of context, these sentences suggest how skillfully Evans is guiding his reader, building bridges for him, persuading him. . . . To repeat the point made a few moments ago: Continuity doesn't magically happen, it's created.

Summary

There are only three steps to writing a good article or speech:

1. Begin with an introduction of your subject at the end of which you announce your organizing idea.
2. Illustrate your organizing idea with details, details, details. This is your evidence which persuades your reader to accept the validity of your organizing idea.
3. End with a conclusion in which you summarize what you've written (briefly), allude back to your introduction, and take your main point a step further.

Of course, the bulk of your paper is Step #2

PUBLISHING ARTICLES

Publishing technical articles is one way industry talks to clients. A company wants certain people to know about the results of its research, because this is a good way to attract new clients as well as to keep old ones.

Why Publish Articles?

Let's look at how this works. Suppose a utility company needs a major new installation. Frequently it will turn to an architectural consulting firm for advice about which architect could best handle the needed installation. The architects who work for the consulting firm will, of necessity, be familiar with all that is going on in their field. One important way they keep up with everything that is going on is by reading all the technical journals which deal with architecture. Obviously, practicing architects, or those in the field, will want the consulting architects to know about their successes.

There is no better way for a firm to advertise its expertise than to publish articles in trade and technical journals. Ads in national magazines and on network radio and TV are scattershot; they may or may not reach the few people who could make a difference. Besides, national advertising is horrendously expensive. How much more efficient to hit the specialized journals.

J. Ray McDermott, one of the largest manufacturers of offshore rigs, places articles in *Offshore Magazine* as often as it can. Right now McDermott is building a new kind of rig called a guide tower. They are the only people in the business doing this, and they want the world to know about it. The best way to let the world know, and by world they mean the world of offshore drilling, is to publish their news in the industry's technical journals.

So, publishing articles in the right places is advantageous to companies; it's also a good way to get ahead for individuals. Putting your expertise on paper for professional journals and trade magazines is an excellent way to get the recognition of people in your field, and that recognition can translate into promotion, raises, or a new job. Lawyers, accountants, economists, marketing and financial executives, doctors, and nurses are highly mobile these days. A by-line in a reputable journal with high professional visibility will give you independence, even within your own company. High professional visibility is as important, and maybe more so, than your school credentials. Few people can write well enough to get published. Show that you can do it and at the same time demonstrate your professional abilities. You might be surprised at the results.

Rena Bartos, a vice-president at J. Walter Thompson, published an article in the *Harvard Business Review*. After "What Every Marketer Should Know About Women" appeared, many advertising people started taking her preoccupation with the special problems of selling to women seriously, and this despite the fact that she had been making speeches about the female market long before the article appeared. There's nothing like a by-line in a prestigious journal.

Nelta Kendell, a student nurse at Nassau Hospital on Long Island worked with pregnant adolescents. She wrote an article, "The Unwed Adolescent Pregnancy: An Accident?" and published it in *Nursing Magazine*. Not only was she asked to submit more articles, but when she went job-hunting after graduation, she discovered that her article had attracted considerable attention.

How to Publish Articles

First of all, you've got to find a subject. Think of a question you'd like to have answered. If there's an issue in your field that you've been wondering about, most likely other people have been too. Read several back issues of the journals in your field and decide where your subject would have the greatest chance of being accepted for publication. When you have picked a journal to try for, notice the style and length of other articles appearing in the journal. If you pay attention, you will be enhancing your chances of acceptance. Finally, query the editor. Perhaps the subject you want to write about has already been covered in a past issue. Needless to say, request clearance to publish about any research your company is engaged in.

Second, be choosy about where you publish. In every field, certain journals are perceived to be better than others. How can you tell which are the best? Notice how well the publication is edited, and find out how easy it is to get a manuscript accepted. The best professional publications are refereed. If they are affiliated with a university, like the *Harvard Business Review*, your submitted manuscript will be reviewed by one or two professors specializing in your field. At nonuniversity publications, the referees will be members of a board of editorial advisors as well as a network of professional specialists to whom papers are sent for review.

The *New England Journal of Medicine*, a weekly magazine written by doctors for doctors, which reveals the best, latest, and most important medical research at hospitals and universities in the United States and Canada, has a small staff of in-house editors who get together every Thursday to determine who will be chosen to appear several months hence in what has become the most renowned general medical bulletin in the world. The journal gets about eighty submissions a week; it can accept only three. The articles which make it to the Thursday meetings have already been subjected to a rugged weeding-out process. Some are rejected right away because the writing is so bad. The rest are sent to two or three of the 1,000 or so doctors listed in the *New England Journal of Medicine*'s index of experts in every conceivable branch of medicine. About half of these submissions are thrown out when the specialists spot flaws. What's left ends up at the weekly editors' meeting. Some manuscripts go back to the writers for revisions. And a few, a precious few, are accepted for publication.

The *New England Journal of Medicine* is so widely read, that any doctor whose findings are published there, is likely to be noticed and taken seriously.

Reasons for Rejection

Recently I was permitted to listen in to the deliberations of an editorial board of a prestigious journal. The most common reasons for rejections of manuscripts are the following:

1. Wrong journal. Doesn't writer read us? How could he have our audience so wrong?
2. Much too long and repetitious. Will be considered again if revised.
3. Boring. I wouldn't read beyond the first page if I saw it in our journal. No concrete evidence.
4. Our outside reviewers split right down the middle. The paper's subjectivity is combined with enough pretentiousness to have duped some reviewers entirely. I knew this guy in graduate school, and we never understood him then, either.

The first writer neglected to identify the reader, that first important step in the pre-writing process. The second writer can easily fix his error.

The third forgot that without precise details, there can be no convincing or interesting evidence; and the fourth used too many abstractions, no doubt the intangible works like love, honor, obedience, and patriotism, for example.

Like all marketable skills and commodities, writing ability is affected by supply and demand. The demand is almost insatiable: hundreds of thousands of people are at this very moment busy at writing articles, memos, letters, reports, pamphlets, public relations releases, bulletins, circulars, advertising copy, and instructions, much of it for publication. The supply, however, is limited: few people write well. Fewer still write well enough for publication. Therefore, published writers are highly visible in any organization.

Notes

1. Richard Mitchell, *Less Than Words Can Say*. Boston: Little, Brown and Company, 1979, p. 108.
2. "Adam Smith" (George Goodman), "Will General Motors Believe in Harmony? Will General Electric Believe in Beauty?" In J. B. Hogins and Gerald A. Bryant, Jr., eds., *Juxtaposition*. Palo Alto, CA: Science Research Associates, 1971, pp. 182–83.
3. Goodman, p. 182.
4. Bergen Evans, "But What's a Dictionary For?" *Atlantic*, May 1962, 57–62.

CHAPTER 3

Informative Writing

Under the classification, informative writing, I will discuss reports, memoranda, and letters, the three most commonly used forms in the everyday work-a-day world. Most people name these types technical writing. I prefer the broader term, informative, because strictly speaking, technical writing is that which is carried on by engineers and scientists. There are plenty of professionals other than engineers and scientists who must write reports, memos, and letters. Members of any professional group—doctors, nurses, lawyers, police officers, federal, state, and city civil service employees, clergymen, social workers—are called upon to produce informative writing.

Informative writing is prose constructed to convey ideas and facts with maximum clarity and authority. Clarity means clarity of purpose and authority is that quality of writing that makes the reader take facts and ideas seriously. The greatest ability any writer can have is the capacity to use the language and the infinite ways material can be organized with such intelligence and flexibility that he or she can undertake virtually any writing task, carrying it through competently. If you have this ability, you can face any writing situation with confidence.

Of course, informative writing is frequently used to persuade.

REPORTS

As Gene Cartwright, a manager at Standard Oil of Indiana, put it, "Companies are built around reports."

A report is an objective, organized presentation of factual information that answers a request or supplies needed data. The report usually serves an immediate, practical purpose; it is the basis on which decisions are made. Generally, the report is requested or authorized by one person, and is prepared for a particular, limited audience.

A report conveys exact or useful information. That information should be presented accurately, clearly, concisely, and objectively.

Information must be verified by tests, research, documentary authority, or other valid sources. Information that is opinion or probability should be distinguished as such and accompanied by supporting evidence.

The crucial question to ask about your report is, how well does the report satisfy the needs of the person or persons to whom it is sent?

Many reports aim at a decision:

What method of desalination is best for use at overseas Air Force bases?

What type of rocket should become the major space exploration vehicle?

What size brakes does a car weighing 2000 pounds and developing 280 horsepower need?

Throughout such reports you will argue. When the argument is over, you will present the decisions or recommendations you believe are best.

Common Types of Reports

There is no uniformity in report classifications. Depending upon the business, industry, or particular branch of government, reports may be classified according to subject matter, purpose, function, length, frequency of compilation, type of format, degree of formality, or method by which the information is gathered. It's unrealistic, then, to draw sharp boundaries between types of reports or to try to cover all the situations and problems involved in report writing. Basically, a report is a report is a report. However, certain types are referred to frequently.

Helpful Advice

(1) Always have in mind a specific reader, real or imaginary, when you are writing a report; always assume he or she is intelligent but uninformed. Ask yourself: who will be the primary and secondary readers of this report? Most reports have several readers. Consider these readers in the order of their importance. For example, the primary readers of an insurance policy are the policyholders. But there are secondary readers also: insurance agents and their employees who have to be able to explain everything in a policy; people who work for state regulatory agencies; lawyers; and sometimes judges.

How will these different readers use your report? Suit the report to its primary use. A policyholder may look at his policy only once, but insurance agents and their employees may read it every day.

What do your readers really know? The more diverse your readers and the more technical your material, the more careful you must be to make the report self-explanatory. Remember also that language and ideas which are familiar to you might be puzzling to readers who don't know your job or profession.

What might the attitude of your readers be to what you write? If you suspect they might be unenthusiastic about what you propose, be careful about the words you choose in writing your report. Most people can write a decent English sentence, but establishing the right relationship with the reader is often tricky. (See the section on tone in Chapter 4 for help in establishing this relationship.)

(2) Before you start to write, always decide what the exact purpose of your report is, and make sure that every paragraph, every sentence, every word makes a clear contribution to that purpose and makes it at the right time.

(3) Once the body of the report is written, the writer can analyze the content and write final headings to identify various parts of the material. If during your research you divided the report into headings, you may use these headings, or a modification of them, in the final report. *These headings are the major difference between reports and other compositions.* They help to subdivide the material for a comprehensive listing in the table of contents and thus provide a quick reference to specific sections of the report. A reader interested in only one or two sections of the report, not the whole report, can rapidly locate these sections. Usually, the word *report* implies that the writer will use captions to simplify the task of the reader.

The Progress Report. The progress report gives information concerning the status of a project which is underway. Employees use a progress report to describe investigations to date either at the completion of each stage or as requested by a supervisor. The progress report keeps supervisory personnel informed so that timely decisions can be made.

The progress report describes previous work on the project, discusses in detail the specific aspects that are currently being dealt with, and often states plans for the future. The three parts of the report, previous work, current work, and future plans, form a natural, sequential order for presenting information.

The Employee Performance Report.   Formal appraisals typically involve an interview with an employee who is up for review, as well as completion of the standard company form, which ranges from a series of checklists to essay questions to blank pieces of paper.

Besides determining salary increases, formal appraisals are also a legal tool for the corporation. They provide a documented record of employee performance. If you've been rating the employee "highly satisfactory" for three years and suddenly you're going to dismiss him, you might get sued. So be careful with the employee performance report; be accurate and objective. Effusions or exaggerations could get you in trouble.

The Process Report.   The process report provides instruction for others as to how to follow some procedure. The instructions can be so simple that a single page would suffice, or be so exceedingly complex that a bookshelf of manuals would be required. The report may be elementary, like how to route memos through a company, or technical, like how to operate machinery or program a computer.

G. B. Harrison, a noted Shakespearean scholar, writes about the importance and difficulty of process writing in his book, *Profession of English:*

> The most effective training (in writing) I ever received was not from masters at school but in composing daily orders and instructions as staff captain in charge of the administration of seventy-two miscellaneous military units. It is far easier to discuss Hamlet's complexes than to write orders which ensure that five working parties from five different units arrive at the right place at the right time equipped with the proper tools for the job. One soon learns that the most seemingly simple statement can bear two meanings and that when instructions are misunderstood the fault usually lies with the original order.[1]

Process writing is hard to do. Once I sat in on a class taught by a young instructor of technical writing in the university where I teach and marveled at how he conveyed this difficulty to his students. He told his class to write a description of how to make a peanut butter and jelly sandwich. After ten minutes, he collected the process papers, and read them, remarkably quickly, then handed them back. He called on a student and asked him to read his paper aloud. As the student complied, the instructor reached into a plain brown bag he had brought to class, pulled out a loaf of bread, jars of peanut butter and jelly, and a knife. Following the directions given by the reciting student, he made a sandwich which had the peanut butter and jelly on the outside of the bread. The next several students gave equally bad directions resulting in peculiar looking sandwiches. The instructor's experiment was effective. The students saw how it is necessary to describe every aspect of a process in the proper order.

If you do not write your instructions simply and clearly, readers will misunderstand them and fail to execute them correctly. Here are some pointers on how to do this:

1. Know your readers.
   If you are providing financial instructions, define debit and credit for the layman; assume an accountant knows the meanings. In other words, all unusual terms should be defined unless they are directed to particular professionals who will know what they mean. *

2. Know your process thoroughly.
   Before you write instructions for something, do whatever it is you are describing. If you are telling readers how to change oil in a car, change the oil in your own car before writing up the process.

3. Write simply and clearly.
   If certain tools are needed, if the weather is important, if specific skills are required, if preliminary preparations have to be made, state all this at the outset.
   Make certain all steps are in chronological order.
   Keep sentences short.
   Keep language simple.
   Write in the imperative voice (i.e., Do this; do that).

4. Test your final draft carefully.
   Carry out your written instructions and see if they work. Then try them out on several people to see if any questions arise.

Good instructions are hard to write.

The Proposal Report.   All projects have to begin somewhere, with someone. Think of the projects and programs that have been started in your own place of work in the past year. Everyone in the office may have been tired of going out for coffee, but not until one individual took it upon himself to present a proposal to the office manager did the place get its own coffee-maker.

Proposals are an everyday necessity. An original suggestion may come from a person, company, or agency that would like someone else to do a job that needs doing. On the other hand, a person, company, or agency that desires additional work may offer to render a service to another. In both cases, a written proposal is required.

A proposal should be clear and brief. Begin with a clearly labeled proposition, a single-sentence statement of the change advocated, demonstrate its validity, provide supporting data, recommend action, indicating very explicitly the action you desire, and get the proper support and concurrences along the way from those individuals and units involved.

Formats for the Report

The format may be prescribed by the person or agency requesting the report; it may be suggested by the nature of the report; or it may be left entirely to the discretion of the writer.

The Long Report.   Keep the following in mind when writing a long report:

1. Letter of transmittal or memo
   Professional reports often pass between people who do not know each other well. The letter or memo serves as an introduction.
2. Preface
   States the subject and purpose of the report.
3. Abstract
   A brief statement of the key information in the report. The abstract should be able to stand alone. In fact, some readers may use it as a substitute for the entire report. Keep it brief—200 to 300 words. Abstracts are difficult to write because so much information must be compressed into so little space. Write it after the report is finished.
   The instructions for abstracting given by The Publication Manual of the American Psychological Association are helpful:

   The abstract allows readers to survey the contents of an article quickly. Because, like the title, it is used by *Psychological Abstracts* for indexing and information retrieval, the abstract should be self-contained and fully intelligible without reference to the body of the paper and suitable for publication by abstracting services without rewriting.

An abstract of a research paper should include statements of the problem, method, results, and conclusions. An abstract of a review or theoretical article should state the topics covered, the organizing idea, the sources used (e.g., personal observation, published literature, or previous research bearing on the topic), and the conclusions drawn.

4. Introduction
   Announce four things:
   Subject
   Purpose
   Scope (how broad or limited your treatment of the subject will be)
   Plan of Development

5. Discussion
   The meat of the report

6. Ending
   Summary and recommendation

7. Mechanical Apparatus
   Title page
   Name of company/person preparing report
   Name of company/persons report prepared for
   Title of report
   Date of submission or publication
   Table of Contents
   List of Illustrations
   Sometimes visual aids can convey factual information better than words.
   Sometimes visual aids can be helpful in simplifying information.
   Sometimes visual aids can reduce textual explanation.
   Sometimes visual aids can arouse needed interest.
   Documentation.
   You should let your reader know who was the originator of an idea you use, and let your reader know where that person's work can be found.
   Good documentation enables your reader to research your subject further.
   You must document any direct quote.

Appendices
The following could go in an appendix:
Case histories; illustrations; copies of letters or leaflets
mentioned in report; samples, photographs, supplementary
tables and figures; lists of personnel; suggested collateral
reading; anything else that is not essential to the sense of
the main report.

The Short Report. In short reports, the organization is not as
formalized as in long reports. Even so, you always tell your reader the
purpose and direction of your forthcoming discussion. For example:

> The purpose of the report is to recommend a change in our method of
> producing mousetraps. This discussion first summarizes our present
> procedures, then highlights some of the problems and weaknesses in
> present production, and concludes with recommendations to correct our
> procedures.

A Sample Report. The sample report which follows is addressed
to seven specific readers. It was read, however, by hundreds of other
readers. People interviewed for the job the report campaigns for were
given copies, for example. Students in the university honors program
were other readers. Because the writer remembered to keep diverse
readers in mind, because she never deviated from her exact purpose, to
persuade university administrators to hire a full-time honors director,
because she used concrete language, because she took care to show
readers exactly where she was going in her argument, and because her
report was attractive to look at, her purpose was accomplished: City
University (a pseudonym) did hire an honors director. There are no
subject headings because there are so many tables. To have added
headings would have made the report too "busy."

	from	Amelie Carroll Coordinator of Honors
Primary readers	to	William Marshall
		Vice Chancellor for Academic Affairs
	re:	Recommendation for a full-time director of honors at City University
	cc:	Marshall Vick, Chancellor James MacArthur, Dean, Junior Division

Carol Brine, Chairperson, University Senate Committee on Student Affairs

Gerald Cray, Vice Chancellor for Student Affairs and Member, Committee on Student Affairs

T. A. FitzSimons, III, Director, Hotel, Restaurant, and Tourism and Member, Committee on Student Affairs

Maria Thorne, Member, Committee on Student Affairs

In February, 1979, the University Senate Committee on Student Affairs issued the following statement:

Writer brings her readers up-to-date making sure they remember she is not the only person in the organization who sees the need for a full-time director. She is wise not to assume that those reading the report will remember the details of the Senate's recommendation.

City University wishes to continue its growth in the area of academic excellence and to attract the best students from the community.

Therefore, we recommend that the existing Honors Curriculum be reformulated and expanded to form a fully developed Honors Program.

We recommend that a faculty director be appointed to this project.

As University Honors Coordinator, I would like to comment on the Committee's proposal and to make a recommendation of my own.

The first paragraph of the committee's statement on honors notes the desirability of City University's continued growth in academic excellence and facility in attracting the best students in the community. No doubt this paragraph was meant as a sweetener for the recommendation which was to follow, for the City University is not growing in academic excellence, if one measure of excellence is a student body prepared for college work, nor is the University attracting the best students in the community. Consider the following:

TABLE I

Students Enrolled at City University with
ACT Composite Scores of 27 or Above

Don't assume your readers know such fine points. Explain everything clearly.

(I use 27 because no honors program I know of accepts students below this figure. Considering a score to 36 is possible, this figure does not strike me as unreasonable.)

NEW ENROLLED STUDENTS

Fall Semester	Total Students Enrolled Who Took ACT Test	Composite Above 27	Percentage 27 or Above
1972	2176	195	9.0
1973	2052	161	7.9
1974	1855	110	5.9
1975	1963	105	5.4
1976	2355	96	4.1
1977	2314	81	3.5
1978	1973	60	3.0

Tables sometimes make points more clearly than straight text.

NOTE: National enrolled student norm (1978) is 10.0%
State enrolled student norm (1977) is 6.1%

TABLE II*
Students Who Sent Scores to City University (Enrolled or Not)

| | | SCORES SENT TO CITY UNIVERSITY | | ENROLLED | |
Year	Total	Composite Above 27	Percentage 27 or Above	Composite Above 27	% of Column 2
1972	6948	558	8.0	195	35.0
1973	6670	580	8.6	161	27.8
1974	7134	512	7.2	110	21.5
1975	6758	481	7.1	105	21.8
1976	7203	456	6.3	96	21.1
1977	6992	360	5.2	81	22.5
1978	7039	360	5.1	60	16.4

documentation

Always explain
implications of any
tables you use.

*The figures for Tables I and II were kindly provided by Junior Division Dean, James MacArthur, based on ACT Profile Reports.
    While the number of City University students who score 27 or above on their ACTs is decreasing, the number of remedial students is rising.

TABLE III*
Students enrolled at City University with English ACT scores of 15 and below. (Any student who scores 15 or below is placed in English 0150 or Remedial English.)

Fall Semester	Total Students Enrolled Who Took ACT Test	English Scores 15 and Below	Percentage of Total
1972	2176	559	25.7
1973	2052	667	32.5
1974	1855	618	33.3
1975	1963	717	36.5
1976	2355	1093	46.0
1977	2314	1131	49.0
1978	1973	870	44.0

TABLE IV*
Students enrolled at City University with Math ACT scores of 18 and below. (A student whose ACT score is in the range of 1-12 is placed in 0106; a student whose ACT score is in the 13-18 range is placed in 0107. Both courses are remedial.)

Fall Semester	Total Students Enrolled Who Took ACT Test	Math Scores 18 and Below	Percentage of Total
1972	2176	1036	47.6
1973	2052	966	47.0
1974	1855	1049	56.5
1975	1963	1148	58.5
1976	2355	1575	67.0
1977	2314	1565	68.0
1978	1973	1385	70.0

documentation

*The figures for Tables III and IV are mine based on ACT Profile Reports.

The university has responded to the changing student body which Tables I-IV describe by offering three courses for students with low ACT scores: Math 0106, Math 0107, and English 0150. When the number of students who must take these courses is added to the number of those who must repeat them, enrollment figures grow dramatically and represent a major financial commitment on the part of the university.

In addition to the remedial offerings, the University supports a learning laboratory staffed by a full-time director, a part-time instructor in English, two part-time teaching assistants in English, and volunteer tutors.

In spite of these efforts on behalf of remedial students, whose numbers swell annually, their drop-out rate is high. Only two studies of double remedial students have been undertaken. One, based on the fall 1971 entering freshmen, showed only 5% still enrolled four years later. The other study was based on the fall 1972 entering freshmen and showed 15% still enrolled four years later. Not quite so dramatic, but disturbing nonetheless, is the drop-out rate of the general student population. Out of 10,105 freshmen, sophomores, and juniors who attended City University in the fall of 1976, for example, only 4,666 returned in 1977. The drop-out rate of honor students is slightly higher than that of the general student population. Between 1973 and 1978 there were 300 students enrolled at City University who received Decennial or High School Honor Awards. (The Decennial student receives $100 a year while attending City University; the High School Honor Award student gets between $1000 and $1200 a year.) Of this group, 157, more than 50%, dropped out of school.

Various studies show that the single most important element in student retention is the establishment of a sense of community during the freshmen and sophomore years. Recently the university has attempted to provide such a sense of community for selected freshmen with the College Life Program. To participate in College Life, a student must have ACT scores that indicate placement in remedial math and English although few students are accepted with ACT scores below 8. Students must attend an orientation program, complete application forms, write a brief autobiography, undergo a half-hour interview, and sign a contract agreeing to spend extra hours in class and to spend extra time being tutored, counseled, and advised. A comparison of the fall 1976 College Life group with a matched sample of non-College Life remedial students is made in the following table:

TABLE V

	College Life	Matched Sample*
Number of students starting Fall, 1976	149	123
Number still enrolled Fall, 1977	94 (63%)	38 (31%)

documentation   *Matched by sex, age, high school, hours carried, and ACT scores.

The difference in retention rates is primarily owing to the sense of community which College Life imparts. Would it not be sensible to provide a similar program for City University's stronger students?

Recruiting better prepared students and offering them an honors program will do much toward reversing the trends I have been writing about.

As a member of the State Honors Council, the Southern Regional Honors Council, and the National Collegiate Honors Council, I have spent the last two years investigating honors programs all over the country. The programs that work have one common characteristic: they are headed by a full-time director.

Presently, City University handles honors like most other universities in the state: it appoints a full-time faculty member to direct the Arts and Sciences Honors courses, and gives him a one course reduction.

The best honors program in the state is at State University. State University, a school with 13,000 students, is the only university in the state which has a full-time director. Dr. Malcolm May was appointed director five years ago. Since that time State University has attracted more than its share of top students—of 1300 incoming freshmen in the fall of 1978, 110 had ACT scores of 27 or higher, 8½% as compared to City University's 3%—and it has a retention rate City University would envy. More impressive is the number of fellowships graduating honor students have won. Seniors graduating in June, 1979 are the first State University students to have experienced four years of an honors program run by a full-time director. For the first time in State University's history, the following national fellowships have been won by current graduating honors students:

> one Danforth Fellowship—only fifty awarded in the country; State University got only one in the state
> one Phi Kappa Phi Fellowship—one of only thirty awarded in the country
> two National Science Foundation Fellowships
> one Truman Fellowship—only one of these is awarded in every state

Writer never deviated from her purpose from start to finish.   It is time for City University to hire a full-time director of honors.

The Do's and Don't's of Report Writing

Reports make up a big part of on-the-job communication. The successful operation of many firms depends on reports that either circulate within the company or are submitted to customers, clients, and others with whom a company does business. It would be difficult, in fact, to find a job in business, the military, or in the professions that did not require, at least on occasion, the writing of reports. The following do's and don't's will help you produce a good report.

DO'S

DO use quantitative measures because they are specific. Adjectives like *significant, excellent, extensive,* and adverbs like *rapidly* and *less* are inexact; *significant* in comparison to what?—*less* in contrast with what?

Wrong	*Right*
A significant increase	a $30,000 (20%) increase
Our costs have increased rapidly	Our costs have increased rapidly, from $100,000 in 1959 to $150,000 in 1964, or 50%
Chances are excellent	Chances are 95% certain
Somewhat less	About 75% of the forecast amount
Extensive repairs	At least $10,000 in repairs

DO give the full name of a company when citing it for the first time. It should read General Motors, not GM. If you will be citing a name several times in your report, use the full name the first time and a common abbreviation thereafter.

The American Society for Testing Materials will become ASTM, for example.

DO be sure to proofread all financial figures and check arithmetic. Also, cross-check your report to ensure that a figure cited more than once is the same whenever it appears.

DO be as specific as possible. Examples:

Wrong: Based on the additional expenditure of research and development dollars, the B-1 will be a viable weapon system in the 1980s.

Right: The B-1 will be an effective weapon system only if the fuel leak problems and on-board computers are fixed.

DON'T'S

DON'T assume that those reading your report know the background of the subject or that they remember the details of a previous report on the same related subject.

DON'T use expressions like:

It is felt that	Indicate whether you feel that way or who does
It is reported	Tell who reported it or where it was seen or heard

DON'T overdo technical terminology or trade names. If a technical term or trade name must be used, give an explanation when it is first used.

Examples:

> An optical laser—a device which generates a high energy light beam.
>
> KOVA, the dispersing agent in the backcoat adhesive, is still giving us trouble.
>
> The computer's core storage (i.e., its memory unit) is not adequate because . . .

DON'T blame technology for making writing complex—blame your own language. Just because technology becomes increasingly complex does not mean writing must follow suit. Read what Saul S. Radovsky, M. D., says in an article in *The New England Journal of Medicine* (1979):

> Progress in medical science, by its branching, has given us more kinds of jargon and fewer who can use or understand it. Our bodies and brains are the most complex items that we know, with more parts, more functions, and more known of them than any of the rest. As knowledge of them expands, the jargons subdivide, and the more subdivisions there are, the fewer who can use or understand them. At the true frontier, only researchers who can translate their jargon into English are read with ease by the rest of us.[2]

Suppose you are a technical editor trying to help pilots write test reports on the F-16 fighter. Your job is to translate technical testing and evaluation performed on the F-16 into words that managers and decision-makers would understand. You know that advances in technology exert pressure for changes in our weapon arsenal, but you also know that technology is not making the decision on whether to spend millions of dollars to purchase F-16 fighters. People are doing that.

DON'T put down all you know about a subject in a report. Keep your report as short as possible. In a fifty-page proposal, the logic is invariably wobbly, and it's hard to hold someone accountable for a number buried deep in appendix 7.

DON'T mislead:

We had a bad year, and that's good. State the facts of your bad year or quarter or project clearly, without euphemisms.

The economy is to blame. It always is, more or less. To blame the economy for your group's bad performance is a little like a batter complaining that he can't hit because the pitcher is throwing curve balls. Management's view is that a good employee is one who is professional enough to adjust to a volatile economy.

Isn't it a beautiful report? Oh, very pretty, but all those beautiful tables, graphs, charts, even photographs, may look good, but without straightforward analysis, of what value are they?

A room addition is not an expansion. A new plant is one thing, but if you've added a few offices here and some shelf space there, don't dwell on it.

Our people are terrific. Give praise where it's earned, but try not to be perfunctory about it. Uninspired expressions of prose can be deadly, whereas an imaginative accolade is remembered and savored.

We're cyclical. Cyclical is a slippery concept. Is cyclical something seasonal or is it something dependent on factors in other industries, other markets, or other economies? Define what you mean.

Strike while the iron is cold. Your division's strong results of last quarter of the preceding year are old news, and unless there is a really good reason for their being re-reported in the present year's report, don't. Otherwise, it looks as if you're trying to hide some less than good news in the present year's report.

REMEMBER: As with every type of writing task, your report will be as good as the preparation that goes into it. The steps outlined in Chapter 1 apply to reports as much as to articles and speeches.

MEMORANDA

The memorandum (memo) is used primarily within the firm. The term *memo* used to mean a communication of a temporary nature, but now refers to any communication which makes needed information immediately available or which clarifies information.

Some companies have printed memo forms, but if yours does not, make your own by typing in these headings:

To:
From:
Subject:
Date:

Like employees elsewhere, most of those who enroll at the Sun Institute for the Sun Company course called "Write Up the Ladder" suffer from a lack of confidence about writing basic memos and letters. "They hate to be straightforward or direct," says George Murphy, one of the Villanova University English professors who handle the course. Says Bonnie Perry, a Sun education director, "Their idea of what constitutes

Memo To Those Who Write Memos:

Art Buchwald tells of the kid who visited his father's office. When asked what his father did, the kid said, "He sends pieces of paper to other people and other people send papers to him." When you draft a memo, remember other people love to "correct" drafts. The more textually taut you keep it, the less chance for others to pounce on it. The Lord's Prayer has 71 words. The Ten Commandments have 297. The Gettysburg Address has 271. The legal marriage vow has two. General McAuliffe at the Bulge made his point in one: "Nuts!" For practice, send your memo to yourself as a straight telegram at your own expense. Chances are, the less your telegram costs, the more effective your memo is.

Courtesy of United Technologies.

good writing is something that is excessively pompous and stilted. They go on and on, never getting to the point." (*Time*, May 19, 1980)

Nearly everyone, Republican and Democrat, liked Hubert Humphrey, yet few admired his verbosity. When Lyndon Johnson was having his kidney operation, the risk of death existed, so Bill Moyers was positioned outside the operating room, in case of such an eventuality. Moyers said to Johnson: "What do I *tell* Hubert?" Replied Johnson: "Tell him to keep it short."

One of the key features of well-managed companies is that they keep things simple in spite of overwhelming pressures to complicate things. Procter & Gamble, for example, is famous for its one-page memo. Besides cutting paperwork, the one-page memo reinforces Procter & Gamble's "action" focus, its no-nonsense approach to management. Writing a short memo is not easy. Chairman Ed Harness says it usually takes at least a dozen drafts for a young recruit to get his first one right. But Mr. Harness argues that this discipline sets the tone for crisp, fact-based analysis: "We don't go in for any of that 'let's get together and rap' nonsense. A brief presentation that winnows fact from opinion is the basis for decision-making around here." (*Wall Street Journal*, October 27, 1980)

LETTERS

The most common of all professional writing forms is the letter. Every day the mails are flooded with several million business letters: letters of inquiry, reply, application, adjustment, recommendation, complaint, invitation, credit, sales, and collection, to mention only a few.

Many business and professional letters are stiff and clichéd. They needn't be. Eliminate hackneyed expressions like:

> I am in receipt of your letter of November 12 . . .
>
> The purpose of this letter is to inform you . . .
>
> Referring to your letter of June 13 . . .

Careless letter-writing wastes time. A manufacturing firm in the Northwest sent out three letters to clarify its original announcement about a new process. If the manager had spent more time with the first letter, there would have been no need for subsequent correspondence. Taking time to write letters well is not squandering time; it's smart time-management.

A good business writer rereads his letter asking, "Will it make friends?" Don't be satisfied with merely avoiding anything offensive; exude warmth, friendliness, sympathy, and goodwill. You do this by relying on works like "please," "thank-you," "I appreciate," "I enjoyed," and the like. Use words with favorable connotation.

> We have received your letter in which you claim the rug was damaged in shipment.

> Thank you for letting us know about your damaged rug.

Claim is slightly insulting. It sounds as if you don't believe the writer is telling the truth.

> Because you failed to include an estimate, we cannot award you the contract.

> Because an estimate was not included, we cannot award you the contract.

Failed is irritating. No one likes to be accused of having failed.

> You must be mistaken about the price, as our records indicate it was $12 a dozen.

> As there is some misunderstanding about the price, please check to see whether they indicate that it was $12 a dozen.

Mistaken isn't pleasant. Find a softer word.

Tips for Writing Good Letters

1. Be clear about what you want to accomplish by your letter—
   get a loan,
   get an interview,
   make a complaint,
   before you begin writing that letter.
2. Address whomever you are writing by name, not Dear Sir, Dear Madam, Ms., or other salutations. Spell the person's name correctly. You can always get someone's name by phoning his or her company, or look it up in a business or professional directory in your library.
3. State what your letter is about in your first paragraph.
4. Be positive even when you have a gripe. Disagreeing agreeably can be learned by everyone. If you explain why a refusal must be made to a request, you will defuse your reader's potential anger.
5. Be natural; talk to your addressee as if he or she were sitting in front of you. Avoid jargon. Read your letter out loud after you have finished writing it. Never try to be cute, funny, or flippant. This will backfire, causing your reader to think you have no sense of discretion.

6. Make your letter look good. Type it on quality 8½" × 11" stationery if it's personal; on company stationery for business. Keep it neat. Of course there should be no typos and no misspelled words.

7. Keep your letter as short as possible.

8. Never exaggerate. Do it once and you've lost all credibility. Your reader won't trust you again.

9. Keep opinions separate from facts. Let your reader know which is which. He'll respect you for it.

10. Edit carefully, deleting all unnecessary words.

11. End by telling your reader just what you want, and tell him or her directly. Don't beat around the bush. "I will be in New York the week of May 4, and would appreciate an interview then. Next Monday, April 20, I'll call your secretary and see when it will be most convenient for you."

12. Close your letter with "Sincerely." Sign your name legibly.

Comparison of a Good and Bad Letter

Now let's look at two letters, both written to the chairman of a search committee for the dean of the College of Liberal Arts at City University. One is clearly better because it *shows* the reader why a certain candidate should be considered. The other *tells* a few things about this same candidate, but shows nothing. Can you determine which is which?

Letter #1

―――――――――――――――――――――――――――――――――――

May 28, 1983

Dr. Conrad Mueller
Chairman, Search Committee
Department of Sociology
City University
City, State 00000

Dear Professor Mueller:

Section one: purpose of letter
　　It is timely, I think, for City University to appoint a woman to a top administrative position. Maria Kelly is the most qualified woman on campus to be the Dean of the College of Liberal Arts.

Section two: her
experience as
assistant to the
Chancellor; very
specific details of
what she did on the
job and what this
experience has to
do with the job
she's applying for
now.

For the past two years, as Academic Assistant to the Chancellor, Dr. Kelly sat in on the Monday morning meetings of the Chancellor and Vice-Chancellors representing the faculty viewpoint on such matters as capital outlay priorities; the Christmas shut-down; the need for an honors director; the Title III grant; the reorganization of Continuing Education, off-campus courses, and City University-Innsbruck into Metropolitan College; the development of off-campus centers; the recruitment of students; and the revamping of orientation. Besides this she handled all faculty grievance procedures, helped pass and implement the City University-Board of Education partnership, was instrumental in getting the College of Business to file a letter of intent for a para-legal program, helped put together the mayoral internship program on campus, advised the Chancellor on the appointment of faculty committees, was chief liaison with the senate policy committee, helped with the revision of the bylaws for the Faculty Council and University Senate, attended all meetings of the State Board of Supervisors, and represented City University at two national meetings of the American Council on Education.

What has all this, impressive as it is, to do with being Dean of the College of Liberal Arts? One of the most important functions of a dean is to relate to higher administration. In this aspect of the job, Maria Kelly has an advantage that no other candidate has. She has been within the inner sanctum of higher administration on this campus. She knows intimately how things are done at that level.

Not only could Maria Kelly serve the College of Liberal Arts in the capacity of liaison between the faculty and higher administration better than any of the other candidates, she also knows the job of dean from "below" as a department chairman, and "at level," as it were, as frequent member and chairman of the Liberal Arts Advisory Committee. No one else has served at all three levels of administration.

Section three: her
experience in the
community; very
specific details as
to what these
experiences were
and how they fit the
job she's applying
for now.

Now that City University's future as a strong urban university seems assured, it is time for the college to have a dean who will be community oriented. Here again, Maria Kelly exhibits an exposure to the world outside City University that no other candidates can match. She is Chairman of the State Committee for the Humanities; she is a board member of the city's public library history program sponsored by the National Endowment for the Humanities; she is Chairman of the Educational Task Force for the city region; and she is Coordinator for the State Planning Commission, National Identification Program of the Office of Women in Higher Education of the American Council on Education. There are other outside activities, but these, the more prestigious, have made Maria Kelly's name known in education circles at the state and national levels.

Section four: her
personal traits
which equip her for
the job she's
applying for.

Besides having outstanding leadership qualities, Dr. Kelly's personal traits will equip her well for the job. She has unerring good judgment and common sense. I have seen her interview as many as a hundred candidates for a job in Political Science in a four-day period, and at the end come up with the handful of best people of the group. I have seen her make difficult decisions because she has an ability to keep her eye on the main element eliminating confusing and sometimes conflicting side issues. I have seen her complete several different chores in one day, in spite of several interruptions, keeping everything straight and not getting rattled. Most importantly, I know her to be a person of the utmost discretion, honesty, and trustworthiness.

Finally, no other candidate knows City University and the State system and how they really work better than Maria Kelly. She will make an outstanding dean.

Sincerely,

Thomas Wade

Thomas Wade
Professor of Political Science

Letter #2

May 28, 1983

Dr. Conrad Mueller
Chairman, Search Committee
Department of Sociology
City University
City, State 00000

Dear Professor Mueller:

I have known Dr. Maria Kelly since 1963 when I joined the faculty of City University. I have served on committees with her, observed her in numerous faculty meetings, and have personal friendship with her.

Dr. Kelly's ability as a teacher and a scholar is without peer, and she has established a solid reputation in the Political Science Department.

Additionally, over the years, she has achieved a great deal of success in the Political Science Department as Coordinator of Undergraduate Studies, as chairman of the Department, and more recently on the university-wide level, as Academic Assistant to the Chancellor.

In all of her activities Dr. Kelly has time and time again demonstrated: a deep commitment to scholarship, an abiding loyalty to the principles of City University as an urban university, a clear understanding of the role this university must play in the community, and a forceful leadership on all levels in diverse and difficult circumstances.

The university could choose no one more able to conduct the affairs of the College of Liberal Arts on a continuing basis, to direct the various programs of the college, and to build for the future.

I recommend her to you without reservation.

Sincerely yours,

Terence Watson

Terence Watson
Professor of Political Science

You should have decided Letter #1 was the better recommendation chiefly because it is specific and concrete about Dr. Kelly's activities and accomplishments. We see that Maria Kelly has had ample experience to direct a college. The letter isn't perfect; the writer does not begin by stating his relationship to the candidate, how long he has known her, under what auspices, and so on (the writer of Letter #2 wisely does this), but perhaps the writer of Letter #1 is assuming that since he is a member of the candidate's own department, the search committee chairman will automatically understand the relationship.

Although the second letter writer got off to a strong start, he slowed down right away. Paragraph two, "Dr. Kelly's ability as a teacher and scholar is without peer, and she has established a solid reputation in the Political Science Department," lacks specificity. We are given no evidence of Dr. Kelly's scholarship (i.e., awards, classes taught, seminars given); and what is a solid reputation? That's vague. (The writer also misused *peer* which means a person who is of equal standing with another. Ability, then, can't be without peer.)

The third paragraph lists Dr. Kelly's three administrative positions, but then says nothing about what kind of job she did in these positions. "A great deal of success" tells us nothing.

The fourth paragraph is pure abstraction:

In all of her activities Dr. Kelly has time and time again demonstrated: a deep commitment to scholarship;

This was mentioned in the second paragraph; no evidence of this commitment is given in either place.

an abiding loyalty to the principles of City University as an urban university;

What is an abiding loyalty? Remember, words like love, honor, patriotism, loyalty are big abstractions and convey almost nothing unless you define exactly what you mean by them. Does anyone at City University, even the Chancellor, know what its principles are? Principles is another slippery word; it's too abstract to stand alone.

a clear understanding of the role this University plays in the community;

What is the role? What is it about the role that Dr. Kelly understands? How do you know that she understands in just this/that way?

a forceful leadership on all levels in diverse and difficult circumstances.

What is forceful leadership (remember it's never been explained or shown), and what does "on all levels" mean? For that matter, what are the "diverse and difficult circumstances?" You don't know and can't know because the writer never told you. He is just using words to fill a page.

The final recommendation that "the University could choose no one more able," has never been demonstrated. Although the writer of Letter #2 meant, no doubt, to help his candidate, letters like this actually do harm. Perceptive readers are apt to think—if this is all X can say about Y, is it because Y isn't all that good? Often the problem is the writer isn't doing his job properly, but unfortunately, his missive is a reflection on his candidate.

And once again: the pre-writing steps outlined in Chapter 1— identifying your reader, limiting your subject, collecting your data, categorizing your data, and finding your organizing idea (or purpose in a report, memo, or letter)—are just as applicable to report, memo, and letter writing as they are to article and speech writing. Without adequate preparation, your memo or letter will be disorganized. Recently, I read a letter of application in which the writer started by asking for a certain job, then jumped forward to his plans for the future, next backed up to early schooling, then went forward to work experience, and so on back and forth with no logical order. Such a letter gives the reader a bad impression of the writer's ability to think clearly principally because it's so disorganized. By contrast, the writer of Letter #1 carefully keeps similar points together: a section on the applicant's experience in higher administration and another on her accomplishments outside the university, for example. Careful preparation will make you well organized, too.

Notes

1. G. B. Harrison, *Profession of English*. New York: Harcourt, Brace & World, Inc., 1962, p. 149.
2. Saul S. Radovsky, M.D., "Medical Writing: Another Look," *The New England Journal of Medicine*, 301, No. 3 (July 3, 1979), p. 131.

CHAPTER *4*

Style

I have a friend who will often say, "I can't do that; it's not my style." I love the expression, and I know exactly what she means. She won't go downtown unless she's dressed up, for example, because that's just the way she is. When we speak of Hemingway's style, we mean the way he puts words together. His spare prose is always recognizable. The way you use language reveals something about you.

Your decision about the language you use is, in part, calculated to present to your reader a recognizable person. Realizing that when you write, something of yourself is escaping into the open, you will want to be conscious of this style which expresses you. You will want to be precise because no one wants to be thought repetitious and boring, and you will want to establish the right relationship with your reader because the wrong tone does more to defeat a writer's purpose than nearly any other fault.

PRECISION

William Strunk, Jr., a long-deceased but still-remembered English professor at Cornell, told his students: "Vigorous writing is concise. A sentence should contain no unnecessary words, a paragraph no **63**

Keep It Simple

Strike three.
Get your hand off my knee.
You're overdrawn.
Your horse won.
Yes.
No.
You have the account.
Walk.
Don't walk.
Mother's dead.
Basic events
require simple language.
Idiosyncratically euphuistic
eccentricities are the
promulgators of
triturable obfuscation.
What did you do last night?
Enter into a meaningful
romantic involvement
or
fall in love?
What did you have for
breakfast this morning?
The upper part of a hog's
hind leg with two oval
bodies encased in a shell
laid by a female bird
or
ham and eggs?
David Belasco, the great
American theatrical producer,
once said, "If you can't
write your idea on the
back of my calling
card,
you don't have a clear idea."

*Courtesy of United Technologies

unnecessary sentences, for the same reason that a drawing should have no unnecessary lines and a machine no unnecessary parts. This requires not that the writer make all his sentences short, or that he avoid all detail and treat his subjects only in outline, but that every word tell."[1]

Bad writers suppose that style is ornamentation. But style is not something separate from that which you write—you can't add style after you've finished to try to "soup it up," the way a hotrodder "soups up" his car by adding extra-big wheels. Style is not the sum total of devices, mannerisms, tricks, and adornments. The way to style is by way of plainness and simplicity.

Ernest Hemingway said, "Writing plain English is hard work." He should know for few did it better. To help you write plain English, keep the following admonitions in mind.

Use Active Verbs

A verb is active when its subject does whatever action the verb is describing. A verb is passive if its subject is acted upon by something else.*

Bobby threw the ball.	*Threw* is an active verb because its subject, *Bobby,* is the one who does the action.
The ball was thrown by Bobby.	*Was thrown* is a passive verb because its subject, *the ball,* is acted upon and does not itself act.

Because the verb is the action word, it is the center of every sentence. It is better, therefore, to keep that action word active. Theodore Bernstein in *The Careful Writer* points out that the *Declaration of Independence* is good prose because of its strong, unequivocal verbs. Of 1500 words in the document, only a dozen verbs appear in the passive form. Others are notably active.

Sometimes it's necessary or desirable to use the passive form of the verb to pass the buck or to avoid responsibility for an action. For example:

It was decided to destroy the evidence.

Who made this decision? We aren't told. The writer hedges either to conceal who decided or to hide the fact that he doesn't know.

*For those who want a quick refresher course in the parts of speech, see the Appendix.

Avoid Stringing Nouns Together

Remember, an adjective modifies a noun; a noun may not be used to describe another noun.

Noun   Noun Noun   Noun

Early <u>childhood</u> <u>thought</u> <u>disorder</u> <u>misdiagnosis</u> is the result of not knowing

Noun   Noun

recent <u>research</u> <u>literature</u> on the problem.

Besides not knowing what's early, the childhood, the disorder, or the diagnosis, the sentence is just plain bad grammatically.

Look at the following abominations:

The plant safety standards committee were against air quality regulation announcements.

The art of cardiac sound interpretation requires an intimate cardiac physiology and cardiac disease pathophysiology knowledge.

Some of writers' greatest follies flow from the fact that they string nouns together. Look at career education, for example. Career education is not training in the necessary skills of this or that career, but information that there are several careers available to any individual. Richard Mitchell in *Less Than Words Can Say* (1979) talks about the idiocy which results from stringing nouns together:

> It's important that both words be nouns. Notice that Religion Education is different from Religious Education, for instance. Religious Education might actually have some subject matter; Religion Education, however, would be aimed not at teaching this or that *about* a religion, but at alerting students to the fact that this or that religion does exist and suggesting how they might want to feel about that. In like fashion, Investment Education, a likely candidate, would not undertake to teach people how to invest. It would reveal that there is such a thing as investing and that it makes America strong. . . . Courses in History Education will not bother students with the terms of the Treaty of Versailles or the details of the growth of American Federalism. They will provide students with a personal appreciation of the fact that there *is* such a thing as history and that we are *all* part of it—isn't that wonderful?
>
> All the educations are strings of words, of course, not things in the world.[2]

Cut Unnecessary Words

Whatever you write, shortening it almost always makes it tighter and easier to read and understand.

The answer ~~does not rest with laziness or dishonesty. It lies largely in~~ *is*
having hired too many people to do the job.

Joseph Williams in his book, *Style* (1981), gives a wonderful example of wordiness:

> The point I want to make here is that we can see that American policy in regard to foreign countries as the State Department in Washington and the White House have put it together and made it public to the world has given material and moral support to too many foreign factions in other countries that have controlled power and have then had to give up the power to other factions that have defeated them.

Which means,

> Our foreign policy has backed too many losers.[3]

One way to cut wordiness is to avoid being redundant. Why say free gift? What other kind of gift is there?
Other redundancies:

full and complete	true facts
willing and able	important essentials
each and every	future plans
first and foremost	personal beliefs
completely finish	sudden crisis
past memories	terrible tragedy
each individual	end result
basic fundamentals	final outcome
	initial preparation

Another way to cut wordiness is to steer clear of the following:

No	Yes
at this point in time	now
finalize the termination of something	end it
at the present time	now
in the event of	if
in the majority of instances	usually
along the lines of	like
for the purpose of	for
in as much as	since, because
in accordance with	by, under

Use Adjectives and Adverbs Sparingly

Keep your adjectives to a minimum. This will simplify your style and force you to find strong nouns.

Don't use the trite adverbs like:

very	quite
really	extremely
rather	terribly
somewhat	

Does "Margot enjoyed a very pleasant day at the beach" convey more than "Margot enjoyed a pleasant day at the beach"?

Refrain from Jargon

Technical, elitist professional jargon accomplishes two things and they are both bad: it intimidates the uninitiated and dodges the subject.

Examples of jargon:

Businessese: The unanticipated rebound in consumer spending in the third quarter of 1979, which more than regained the ground lost in the second quarter's decline, has combined with the shift in monetary policy announced in early October to change significantly the configuration of economic activity during 1980, although the full year results will not differ greatly from the forecast issued in September as part of the long range plan background material.

Academese: A professor of education described what he and his colleagues did for students who took their courses as "credentialing relevant competencies." Another university professor, describing the aims of his field, wrote: "A topian educational system of values and its existing isomorphic formulated goals and means can be traumatically challenged by EE (Environmental Education) and its evolving, diverse-goal system as EE functions as a catalytical non-discipline to prepare and facilitate people to move through a meta-transition into the phase of non-stationary culture."

Officialese:

The following is a passage from a document called "Draft Regulations to Implement the National Environmental Policy Act." "The agency need make the finding of no significant impact available for public review for thirty days before the agency makes its final determination whether to prepare an environmental impact statement and before the action may begin only in one of the following limited circumstances: . . . "

Medicalese:

A doctor who manages a hospital wrote this: "The evaluation strategy is to implement evaluation in methodologies which will provide assistance to the conceptualization of issues, the ascertainment of perceived priorities, and more importantly, the formulation of rationale and impetus for constructive cooperative planning."

Legalese:

The following is taken from an out-of-date loan application form from First National City Bank of New York: "A fine computed at the rate of 5 cents per $1 on any installment which has become due and remained unpaid for a period in excess of 10 days, provided (A) if the proceeds to the borrower are $10,000 or less, no such fine shall exceed $5 and the aggregate of all such fines shall not exceed the lesser of 2 percent of the amount of this note or $25, or (B) if the annual percentage rate stated above is 7.50 percent or less, the limitations provided in (A) shall not apply and no such fine shall exceed $25 and the aggregate of all such fines shall not exceed 2 percent of the amount of this note, and such fine(s) shall be deemed liquidated damages occasioned by the late payment(s) . . ."

The examples of businessese, academese, officialese, medicalese and legalese are sterile and incomprehensible in their jargon, not to mention absurd in their pomposity. It is all impenetrable language, characterized by big words, serpentine phrases, prefabricated expressions, grammatical infractions, convoluted syntax, and plain illogic.

Dr. Lois DeBakey's term for the linguistic ailment that afflicts doctors is *medicant*. Dr. DeBakey, Professor of Scientific Communication at Baylor College of Medicine at Houston, has been fighting medical gobbledygook for years, along with her sister, Selma, and her brother, famed heart surgeon Michael DeBakey. When speaking at Tulane University recently she said, "My files are bulging; they are absolutely crowding me out of my office." What they are bulging with are classic examples of bad writing by doctors and nurses. Some of her favorites:

> The intern had noted that the patient was unresponsive in bed.
>
> A pelvic examination was done on the floor.
>
> Have you done a urine on him?
>
> It was decided to explore this patient.

Medicant is by no means limited to those who take the Hippocratic oath. It strikes politicians, lawyers, engineers, clergymen, academics; jargon turns up in every profession, so much so that some states have enacted Plain English Laws. The aim of any Plain English Law is to free consumers from decades of garble which lawyers have built into ordinary, everyday transactions. Apartment leases, time purchase agreements, small loan applications, and car payment contracts come under the new law's scope.

Someone applying for a loan at Citibank (the First National City Bank of New York) will find he or she is in default if: "(1) I don't pay an installment on time, or (2) if any other creditor tries by legal process to take any money of mine in your possession." The example replaces a 117-word paragraph, filled with words like: the undersigned, covenant, evidencing, distraint proceedings, and Uniform Commercial Code. The New York Plain English Law says: "Every written agreement" up to $50,000, where the transaction is for personal, family, or household purposes, must be "written in a clear and coherent manner using words with common everyday meanings."

The Internal Revenue Service has hired Alan Siegel, the man who redesigned Citibank's Consumer loan forms, to simplify tax forms. If all goes according to plan, the federal income tax return will be written in simple English. Siegel wants better explanations of terms like dividend exclusion, adjusted gross income, and earned income credit that confuse many people. "If you simplify, you cut down on the amount of paperwork and you free up the time of the employee and the customer," he said. "And once one form changes, all others must in order to conform." (*The Times Picayune*, Dec. 21, 1980)

Susan Hecht, head of a communications consulting firm, shows how to translate gobbledygook into simple sentences. Following is a bank form about a lost passbook:

> Said passbook or the said account or any interest therein has not been sold, assigned, transferred, pledged, or hypothecated.

Translated into simple English, it becomes:

> I have not used the account as security for a loan, or transferred it, or part of it, to anyone else.

Following is another bank form:

> In the event that said account shall be overdrawn as a consequence of checks drawn or withdrawals made by any of us, we jointly and severally agree to reimburse bank for the amount of such overdraft, regardless of the manner in which or by whom the same may have been caused.

Translated into simple English, it becomes:

> We are all responsible for reimbursing you for overdrafts, no matter who of us causes them.

Following is an automobile lease:

> There are no warranties, express or implied, by lessor or lessee, except as contained herein, and lessor shall not be liable for any loss or damage to lessee or to anyone else of any kind and howsoever caused, whether by any vehicle leased hereunder or the repair, maintenance or equipment thereof or by any failure thereof or interruption of service or use of any vehicle leased hereunder.

Translated into simple English, it becomes:

> A warranty is a kind of guarantee given to stand behind a product and its performance for a certain length of time. I agree that the only warranties I receive under this lease are written here.

Eliminate Clichés

Clichés are phrases that have been dulled by repetition. Unless you want your writing to sound dull, eliminate them.
Examples:

"good as gold"	"wrack and ruin"
"heart of gold"	"nipped in the bud"
"sly as a fox"	"at this point in time"
"spur of the moment"	"straight from the shoulder"
"not my cup of tea"	"by and large"
"fresh as a daisy"	"raining cats and dogs"
"dull as dishwater"	

Shun Euphemisms

The frightened PR men of the nuclear power industry won the 1979 doublespeak award of the National Council of Teachers of English for a retreat into euphemism during the near-disaster at Three Mile Island. In their lexicon, an explosion became an "energetic disassembly" and fire was transformed into "rapid oxidation." Plutonium didn't contaminate things; it became a friendly little substance that "took up residence."

Government bureaucrats are always inventing euphemistic phrases for unsatisfactory conditions, phrases that gloss over the facts. Examples:

developing nations	house of correction
senior citizens	intelligence gathering operations
substandard housing	

Instead of	**Why Not**
redeployment of troops	withdrawal
nonwhites in a culturally deprived environment	blacks living in slums
pacification of the enemy infrastructure	blasting the Viet Cong out of a village
final solution	death of 6,000,000 humans in gas ovens
dentures	false teeth
disadvantaged/ underprivileged	poor
secure employment	get a job
personal preservation flotation devices	life jackets

TONE

People write in "businessese," "academese," "officialese," "medicalese," and "legalese" because someone (teacher? mentor?) has taught them that informality is unacceptable. Writing an informal style is easy—you just talk on paper. Writing a formal style is simple too—you elevate your diction, assume a grave manner, and use elaborate sentences; you try, in short, to imitate what you think is a lofty, formal style. Each style has its drawbacks. Informal style, like conversation, tends to be loose, banal, and imprecise. You'll sound natural all right, but not terribly bright. But using formal style isn't the answer because if you're like most people, you'll produce it by hauling out all the highfalutin phrases you've ever heard.

Finding the Right Mix of Formal and Informal

Style doesn't have to be informal or formal. Between the two extremes of lofty and colloquial, there is a middle style, a compromise between the two. Achieving the middle ground is tricky because it presupposes a sophisticated control of tone. You've got to get the right mix of the two extremes and you've got to suit your style to the task at hand. Knowing how to mix and how to suit it to the purpose of your writing are matters of a good ear, taste, and tact. Developing a good ear, taste, and tact is directly dependent on the kind and amount of reading you do. The kind of styles of *Harper's Magazine*, *The Atlantic Monthly*, *Newsweek*, the editorials of *The New York Times*, and *The Wall Street Journal* are examples of a good mix of the lofty and colloquial. All show a movement toward greater naturalness. They all permit contractions, for example. So the mix definitely leans toward the colloquial. You'll always strive to sound natural, leaning toward a colloquial style, but you'll learn how to adjust the degree of colloquialism depending on the audience for whom your work is intended.

Here are two short examples. The first is a paragraph from a newspaper column; its tone is chatty and casual. The second is a paragraph from the prologue of a biography of Henry Ford; its tone is more formal befitting a full-scale biography of a man of the stature of Henry Ford.

Paragraph #1

In the accompanying example, note the deliberate word choices which make the tone of the piece chatty and casual. These choices fall into three categories: (1) The use of the first person pronoun (underlined). If you want to be more formal use the third person only (he, she, it, they). (2) The use of contractions (enclosed in boxes). (3) The use of slang words or words that verge on slang (circled).

"A Stock Market (Junkie) Confesses"

I play the stockmarket. I've bought stocks outright and on margin, sold them short, owned bonds, (dabbled) in options, speculated in corn, soybeans, soybean meal, soybean oil, wheat, potatoes, iced broilers, live cattle, and sugar. I've paid for all sorts of advisory services, having at one time or other subscribed to *Standard and Poor's Outlook, The Value Line Investment Survey, Barrons, Forbes, Financial World, Business Week, Money,* any number of expensive newsletters, and always, *The Wall Street Journal.* I've listened to brokers from Merrill Lynch, Paine Webber, Dean Witter Reynolds, the old Francis I. Dupont, White Weld, and our own Howard, Weil, Labouisse and Friedrichs. I've even been the recipient of ("hot" tips) from the managing partner of a prestigious Wall Street investment banking house, the president of one of the largest banks in America, and the founder of the most successful hedge fund in the country. I listened to them all. And I've lost money. Why? Is it that (tough) in the market?[4]

Paragraph #2

The tone of this piece is more formal and serious than the preceding one. Note that there are no first person pronouns, no contractions, and no slang words.

The Ford family came from farming stock. The attraction of Michigan for them was a rich soil; as a kinsman had written in 1835, the loam was eighteen inches deep. Though Protestant, the Fords had been tenant farmers in Ireland, tilling the land they lived on for English landlords. And because of English laws, there was no hope that they would ever be anything but tenants. The miracle of America was neither the rich soil nor the absence of potato blight, but that here was a place where a farmer could own the land he worked. Accordingly, William's father bought eighty acres near Dearborn for $350 in 1848. He and his sons literally carved their farm from the forest: ash, birch, cedar, elm, hickory, maple, oak, pine, and walnut trees rose above the tangled undergrowth of the fertile land. Ten years later William bought forty of these cleared acres from his father for $600, and not long after, married Mary Litogot. The newlyweds settled on Mary's family's farm, eventually buying its ninety-one acres. William Ford, whose father and grandfather and great-grandfather had been tenant farmers in Ireland, had a reverence for landownership, which gave him an independence he would never have known in Ireland. This being so, it was a disappointment for William that on the chilly morning of December 1, 1879, his oldest son, Henry, only sixteen, left the farm for the city of Detroit and its factories.[5]

Ways to Establish Tone

Business and professional people often say that they have been put off by the tone of a memo or an article only to meet the author later and find him or her surprisingly gracious or likeable. Tone is important.

By the Words You Choose.   The words you choose will set the tone of what you write. Look at the difference, for example, between the phrases "basically disagree" and "hostile to." Their meaning is close; their tone is miles apart. Examine the following sentences:

"The major powers could exploit their lust for power to so grievous an extent that the world as a whole is thrown into jeopardy."

and

"Any great power can translate its disagreement with another power, whatever the merits of that disagreement, into terms of worldwide trouble."

In the first sentence, "exploit," "lust for power," "to so grievous an extent," and "jeopardy" are emotionally charged words, and used, no doubt, because they convey crisis. The second sentence, although its meaning is similar to the first, contains words which deliberately defuse this sense of crisis—"translate its disagreement" and "worldwide trouble" are good examples.

Thus, the words you use to carry meaning will also convey tone. Let's assume you want to put warmth into a letter. Words like "appreciate," "pleasure," "you," "successful," "delighted," and "rewarding," will aid you. Or perhaps you will have to tell another person that he or she didn't get the job, or that you expect improvement, or that you have to turn down a request. Of course you explain why without apologizing, but all the while accenting the positive elements of the situation or person. These are occasions when you must be sensitive to the nuances of words.

Tact is important, too. Can you discover the right level of deference to use when addressing superiors? If a subordinate fails to recognize his role and writes in a brash tone, he is almost certain to bring trouble on himself. There are word choices he may make throughout his writing that indicate either too great a desire to impress the boss or an insecurity which imparts a feeling of fearfulness, defensiveness, or truculence before authority.

While the subordinate who writes upward in the organization must use tact, supervisors who write down must use diplomacy. If they are overbearing or insulting (obviously without meaning to be), they limit the effectiveness of their management. And because they write as the representative of the company, they can cause serious damage by a careless message. Such carelessness has started strikes and other corporate human relations problems.

Read whatever you've written aloud. This will help keep it sounding natural. If things sound dull and heavy, ask yourself how you would speak the thoughts you want to convey to a friend. On the other hand, guard against sounding too breezy or casual. Of course, ultimately, your tone must be appropriate to the audience for which your writing is intended.

By the Sentence Construction You Use.   Obviously word choice—personal pronouns, contractions, slang, emotionally charged or neutral words—makes a difference in the tone of a piece. Rhetorical techniques can also alter tone. The length of sentences and the way clauses are constructed make a difference (see Chapter 5 for sentence types). You can adjust the formality or informality of your tone by shifting main ideas to the beginning or end of a sentence. Depending on their position, the sentences are classified as loose or periodic. Loose sentences are ones in which the main idea appears first.

Interest rates are high because the federal deficit is huge.

Loose sentences are casual in tone because most people state what they are talking about immediately (subject-verb), qualifying it afterward with modifying phrases and clauses.

In the periodic sentence, the main idea appears at the end, near the period.

If fiscal restraint does not materialize, and if credit is tightened, interest rates will rise.

Periodic sentences can have fairly elaborate subordinate clauses, and then, finally, at the very end of the sentence, comes the main subject-verb pattern. In the loose sentence, important ideas appear first, thus conveying a feeling of naturalness and directness. But in the periodic sentence where the idea is withheld, the tone is more formal because the normal sentence pattern is modified.

Another structural device which lends formality to writing is parallel structure. Comprised of two or more parts, each with similar structures, the balanced sentence eloquently states a comparison or contrast.

> Ask not what your country can do for you—ask what you can do for your country.
>
> President John F. Kennedy

> Men are men before they are lawyers or physicians or manufacturers; and if you make them capable and sensible men, they will make themselves capable and sensible lawyers and physicians and manufacturers.
>
> John Stuart Mill

Walker Gibson, an author of several excellent books on tone, analyzed speeches given by the presidential candidates in the 1980 campaign. His analysis illustrates the difference rhetorical techniques make in tone.[6]

Let's look at the speeches Gibson dissected. This is Ronald Reagan:

> When the New Deal was riding high with a program of social experiments, Mr. Democrat himself, Al Smith, went on nationwide radio to tell his fellow Americans that he could no longer follow the leadership of the party which he had served for twenty years. He said he was taking a walk and he asked the Democrats to look at the record. It is time now for all of us to look at the record, the record of Democratic leadership.

Gibson says:

> [Look at] that first great big fat clause, "When the New Deal was riding high with a program of social experiments." We call that in the trade a left-branching subordination, which simply refers to subordination before you get to the main subject/verb of the sentence. Now in oral language, we utter a subject/verb, more or less in the way I am doing in this very sentence I am now trying to utter, and then we go on adding clauses and reservations and qualifications and other subordinations, in the way I am now doing, because we don't quite know where the sentence is going to end. As we talk, we slam a subject and a verb out there and then we go on. Not so in writing—and here's one of the important distinctions—for when we write, of course, we can fiddle around. We can decide, maybe, to take that right branch I just spoke aloud and make it a left branch, put it ahead of the subject and verb, to add a little elegance, perhaps, to the sentence. In any case, I doubt very much that anyone would talk, off the cuff at least, in quite the syntactical structure that you see there in Reagan's first sentence. It's also, of course, a very long sentence. When we finally do get to the subject, notice that we have to wait a bit before we get to the verb

because of the appositive in "Mr. Democrat himself, Al Smith." Ask yourself if you've ever heard anybody talk that way. We just don't use appositives quite that way in oral language. Reagan continues: Al Smith "went on nationwide radio to tell his fellow Americans," and then come two quite elaborate clauses, "*that* he could no longer follow the leadership of the party, *which* he had served for twenty years." As I said, that's perfectly easy to follow, but it's a pretty windy sentence. His next sentences, of course, are much simpler.

Then Gibson looks at Ted Kennedy's rhetoric:

> Too often in this campaign we have heard easy and expedient nonsense, on the one side, that voting for a particular candidate is somehow a singular proof of patriotism or, on the other side, that we can have higher military spending, lower income taxes, a lower federal deficit, no inflation and no cutbacks in social programs all at the same time. Such appeals to popular frustration confuse rhetoric with reality. They treat implausible slogans as possible solutions, but none of this will relieve any of our problems; much of it will only deepen them.

Gibson's analysis:

> What we have here is a great, big chunk of parallel structure.

> "On the one side, that voting for a particular candidate," blah, blah, blah, and "on the other side, that we can have" blah, blah, blah. Now, again, a parallel structure is pretty hard to produce in the oral language, and it's pretty hard to follow when you're listening to it. And this is quite a chunk of language. That first paragraph is all one sentence, and it really is an example of the sort of syntax that we associate with relatively academic kinds of prose.... And then, the next sentence makes its pitch almost entirely with abstract nouns. Look at those nouns: appeals, frustrations, rhetoric, reality, solutions, problems. There are no people in language like that. The subject of the sentence is "appeals," not the people who are making the appeal. When you say "such appeals confuse rhetoric with reality," you are establishing distance between yourself and the people who are doing it. And if you continue to do that long enough and consistently enough, you eventually create a kind of impersonal voice in your own speaking tone.

Finally, Gibson looks closely at part of a George Bush campaign speech:

> I urge you, first of all, go to the polls and vote. Drag, kicking and screaming, if you have to, your friends to the polls and vote. That is No. 1. You know,

I get so tired of the cynics, people who say nobody can make a difference any more.

You know; you see the problem. You see the problems of the economy, tripling and almost quadrupling the rate of inflation. You know what I am talking about when I talk about that paycheck just not making it.

Gibson concludes:

I trust you see immediately what an astonishing difference this is ... "I urge you first of all to go to the polls and vote." Now right away you notice that that's our first appearance of our first person singular pronoun, and it's our first appearance of a second person pronoun. Interesting, isn't it? The *I*'s and the *you*'s are completely omitted by our professorial voices in the earlier examples, but with Bush we're suddenly moving in with a personality addressing a named audience, *you*. "Drag, kicking and screaming if you have to"—that's not very funny, but at least it's a little bit of a lightening of the tone ... There is also a simple statistical game you can play with this passage. How many sentences are there here compared with the other two? Well, a whole lot of them. And the sentence structure? Very simple, of course.

You can find out something about the presidential candidates by undertaking a study of the styles with which they addressed their audiences. But this isn't the point. If you're aware of the tone people use when they write or talk, you'll most likely begin to pay attention to your own. And you'll be able to adjust your tone to fit your audience. If you show up at a party dressed inappropriately, you know it, and are embarrassed. You know not to wear a sports coat or Bermuda shorts to a formal ball, but there are other occasions when you're not sure how to dress. It's the same with tone which you must adapt to each particular writing event. If you adapt appropriately, you'll sound natural.

Sounding Natural

Being natural does not mean being flip. William Strunk, Jr. and E. B. White have a beautiful example of flippancy in their book, *Elements of Style* (1979):

Well, chums, here I am again with my bagful of dirt about your disorderly classmates, after spending a helluva weekend in N'Yawk trying to view the Columbia game from behind two bumbershoots and a glazed cornea. And speaking of news, howzabout tossing a few chirce nuggets my way?[7]

"Cutesy" is as unacceptable in an alumni(ae) magazine as it is in business and professional writing. The reason it's so offensive is it's completely inappropriate to any situation.

Being natural means avoiding pompous diction like:

pursuant to the recent memorandum
please be advised
in reference to your
"the writer"
"one"
"this author"
"we"

Say "I" if you mean "I," and "we" only when there really is more than one of you involved in the writing.

Use words you are comfortable with; don't overwrite; skip the ornate flourishes; follow these suggestions and you won't sound pompous or stilted.

Winston Churchill wrote, "We shall fight on the beaches, we shall fight on the landing grounds, we shall fight in the fields and in the streets, we shall fight in the hills." (Churchill, 1949)

He could have written instead, "Consolidated defensive positions and essential preplanned withdrawal facilities are to be provided in order to facilitate maximum potentialization for the repulsion and/or delay of incursive combatants in each of several residential categories of location deemed suitable to the emplacement and/or debarkation of hostile military contingents." But of course, he didn't. Churchill perceived early in life that the mastery of the English language would be his staircase to greatness and power. He developed that mastery and wielded it to advance his career and defend the West. And his speeches changed history. His iron curtain speech shifted the opinion of the free world. At the time, we believed that the Soviet Union was our ally and that the United Nations could stop any future wars. But then Churchill made that speech: "From Stettin in the Baltic, to Trieste in the Adriatic, an iron curtain has descended across the continent of Europe."

The best tone is achieved by prose that is direct and concrete. It's like a good firm handshake; it inspires confidence. Bad prose is roundabout and vague; like a limp handshake, it implies insecurity. George Orwell, in his famous essay, "Politics and the English Language" (1940), complained that the whole tendency of modern prose is away from concreteness. To make this point, he translated a passage of good English into modern English.

Ecclesiastes	**Modern English**
"I returned and saw under the sun, that the race is not to the swift, nor the battle to the strong, neither yet bread to the wise, nor yet riches to men of understanding, nor yet favour to men of skill; but time and chance happenth to them all."	"Objective consideration of contemporary phenomena compels the conclusion that success or failure in competitive activities exhibits no tendency to be commensurate with innate capacity, but that a considerable element of the unpredictable must invariably be taken into account."[8]

This is Orwell's account of the translation:

> This is a parody, but not a very gross one. . . . The beginning and ending of the sentence follow the original meaning fairly closely, but in the middle the concrete illustrations—race, battle, bread—dissolve into the vague phrase "success or failure in competitive activities." . . . Now analyze these two sentences a little more closely. The first contains forty-nine words but only sixty syllables, and all its words are those of everyday life. The second contains thirty-eight words of ninety syllables; eighteen of its words are from Latin roots, and one from Greek. The first sentence contains six vivid images, and only one phrase ("time and chance") that could be called vague. The second contains not a single fresh, arresting phrase, and in spite of ninety syllables it gives only a shortened version of the meaning contained in the first. Yet without a doubt it is the second kind of sentence that is gaining ground in modern English.[9]

Orwell wrote those words in 1940.

By now you have undoubtedly faced the fact that a simple, clear style is not your "mother tongue"; it is something that must be worked for. Yet you know you must write; you want to be well thought of; so striving to produce writing that is a pleasure to read is worth all the effort. Through words on the page, writer and reader enter a relationship, one in which the personality of each, real or assumed, is engaged with that of the other. The way you make your personality known is by the tone you adopt in what you write.

Notes

1. William Strunk and E. B. White, *The Elements of Style*. New York: Macmillan Publishing Company, p. xiv.

2. Richard Mitchell, *Less Than Words Can Say*. Boston: Little, Brown & Co., 1979, p. 135.

3. Joseph Williams, *Style*. Glenview, IL: Scott, Foresman and Company, 1981, p. 34.

4. Carol Gelderman, "A Stock Market Junkie Confesses." *Gambit*, December 8, 1980, p. 23.

5. Carol Gelderman, *Henry Ford: The Wayward Capitalist*. New York: Dial Press, 1981, p. 3.

6. Walker Gibson, "The Rhetoric of the 1980 Election." *Louisiana English Journal*, Fall 1981, pp. 1–9.

7. Strunk and White, p. 73.

8. George Orwell, "Politics and the English Language." In Michael J. Hogan, ed., *Words and the Writer*. Glenview, IL: Scott, Foresman & Co., 1983, p. 223.

9. Orwell, pp. 223–24.

CHAPTER 5

Usage

THE SENTENCE AND THE PARAGRAPH

There are three kinds of sentences. The *simple* sentence is one in which some agent acts on some object or person or is acted on by it.

> Babe Ruth hit a home run in the third inning.

The *compound* sentence consists of two simple sentences that are put together.

> Babe Ruth hit a home run in the third inning, and Ty Cobb hit one in the fourth.

The *complex* sentence is made up of two parts, of which the main one is a simple or compound, and the other is a group of words that could not stand alone yet has a subject and verb and contributes to the total meaning.

> Although Babe Ruth was to play seven more innings before the game was over, he could not hit another home run.

The part of the sentence, "although Babe Ruth was to play seven more innings before the game was over," is called a subordinate clause. A subordinate clause (also called a dependent clause) has a subject and verb, but by itself is not a sentence. It must be joined to a sentence by a connecting word (in this case, "although"). The part of the sentence to which the subordinate clause is joined is called an independent clause because it can correctly stand alone ("he could not hit another home run").

If all your sentences are the same length, your writing will be monotonous. You can spot this fault by reading what you've written aloud. If the rhythm is repetitive, then break your sentences up or combine them or extend them.

Several simple sentences strung together make prose fast-paced. Michael Adelstein gives an example of this in his excellent book, *Contemporary Business Writing* (1971):

> Advertisements and other copy necessitating fast-paced prose should consist mainly of simple sentences. They are concise. They strike the reader directly. Like short jabs, their impact is dazzling. They are crisp and clear. Nothing interferes with their message. Nothing slows the reader. His eyes race down the page. Suddenly, when a complex sentence breaks the rush of simple sentences, the reader is forced to slow down, to pause, and perhaps to ponder the implications of what he has read before moving on.[1]

The compound sentence is a pattern we use frequently in conversation because *and* is the first connective that comes to mind to link ideas. This pattern is casual and should not be used much in writing.

The complex sentence signals a precise relationship between ideas. Few of us in speaking have the mental agility to formulate, articulate, and structure our thoughts simultaneously. But in writing we can and must do it. In complex sentences you subordinate one or more minor idea(s) to a major one. You need to use complex sentences frequently in your writing.

The paragraph develops one idea which may or may not be stated as a topic sentence. Below is a paragraph from *The Baker World,* Baker Oil Tools, Inc., which is a development of the first sentence.

> The arithmetic of searching for oil is stark. For all his scientific methods of detection, the only way an oilman can actually know for sure that there is oil in the ground is to drill a well. The average cost of drilling an oil well is over $100,000, and drilling a single well may cost over $1,000,000. And once the well is drilled, the odds against its containing any oil at all are 8 to 1.

You know that a good paragraph has unity, but do you know how long a paragraph should be? There are two reasons for paragraphing: It breaks the material of your article or report into logical units and it creates physical breaks on the page which visually assist the reader. There is no prescribed length. Theodore Bernstein, the arbiter of usage for *The New York Times* says:

> One cannot be arbitrary about paragraphing. It is a means of grouping thoughts, but much more is a visual device. Much depends on the subject, the typography, the purpose of what is being written, the readers to whom it is addressed, and the conditions under which they are likely to read it.[2]

It's even permissible to have a one-sentence paragraph, perhaps to emphasize a crucial point that might otherwise be buried. The one-sentence paragraph is a valuable device, but don't overdo it as it is a dramatic device.

Don't be afraid to make, from time to time, one paragraph five or six lines long and the next 25 or 26. The aim is not uniformity; the aim is to reproduce in visual form the contours of each part of your main idea. A difference in length will contribute to variety and will help sustain interest.

GRAMMAR

A writer can accidentally obstruct a reader's ability to understand a written message by bad grammar. Remember the story in Chapter 1 of the professor who lost a grant because she misplaced a modifier? She wrote, "These two projects have grown out of my dissertation which I will finish this summer," when she meant, "These two projects, which I will finish this summer, have grown out of my dissertation." The reason to strive for correct grammar—and I define grammar as the ways in which words are tied together to transmit meaning from the writer's mind to the reader's, including the ways of indicating what the subdivisions in a sentence can be and where they start and stop—is that errors wrench the reader's attention from the meaning and force it to focus instead on the smaller elements that were never meant to show. You want your reader to be concerned with what you're saying, your content, and your reader will automatically do so unless forced to pay attention to something else.

What follows is a little grab-bag of grammatical rules which many people seem to have forgotten or never really learned in the first place.

This is not a summary of the major grammatical practices in English for such has been treated elsewhere. The *Prentice-Hall Handbook for Writers* and the *Harbrace College Handbook* are excellent sources for such material. For further help on questions of usage, I recommend Theodore Bernstein's *The Careful Writer* (1965), Bergen and Cornelia Evans' *A Dictionary of Contemporary American Usage* (1957), H. W. Fowler's *A Dictionary of Modern English Usage* (1965), Wilma and David Ebbitt's *Writer's Guide and Index to English* (1982), William Strunk, Jr., and E. B. White's *The Elements of Style* (1979), and Rudolf Flesch's *The Art of Readable Writing* (1962).

Agreement

Pronouns should agree in number with the noun or pronoun they refer to:

Each pronoun should agree with *its* antecedent.
(Both *pronoun* and *its* are singular.)

EXAMPLES:

INCORRECT: Did anyone leave their books in the room?

CORRECT: Did anyone leave his or her books in the room?

INCORRECT: In Louisiana they produce a lot of gas.

CORRECT: Louisiana produces a lot of gas.

INCORRECT: Modern man is often more interested in their career than in their family.

CORRECT: Modern man is often more interested in his career than in his family.

A relative pronoun (who, which, that) takes either singular or plural verbs depending upon whether its antecedent (the noun to which it refers) is singular or plural.

EXAMPLES:

He is an employee who takes work home at night.

He is one of those employees who take work home at night.

A verb must agree with its subject. A singular subject requires a singular verb; a plural subject requires a plural verb. Do not let intervening phrases and clauses mislead you.

> The use of drugs, although they offer unquestionable benefit, often result in unfortunate side effects.

must be changed to:

> The use of drugs, although they offer unquestionable benefit, often *results* in unfortunate side effects.

This is because the singular verb *results* must agree with the singular subject of the sentence, *use*, not with the plural subject of the preceding clause, *they*.

> OTHER EXAMPLES:
>
> Only one of the emergency lights was functioning when the accident occurred.

The subject is *one*, not *lights*.

> The advice of two engineers, one lawyer, and three executives was obtained before making a decision.

The subject is *advice*, not *engineers, lawyer*, and *executives*.

> A series of meetings was held to decide the best place to position the ad.

Words like *series, type, part, portion* take singular verbs even when such words precede a phrase containing a plural noun.

> Twenty dollars is the wholesale price of each unit.

Subjects expressing measurement, weight, or mass take singular verbs even though the subject word is plural in form. Such subjects are treated as a unit.

Faulty Parallelism

Faulty parallelism results from joining unlike structures when their grammar or meaning indicates they should be identical in form.

> EXAMPLES:
>
> INCORRECT: Tom is not a good tennis player, and neither is his swimming good.
>
> CORRECT: Tom is not a good tennis player, nor is he a good swimmer.
>
> INCORRECT: She liked the lawn and gardening.
>
> CORRECT: She liked tending the lawn and gardening.

INCORRECT: "We used to root for the Indians against the cavalry, because we didn't think it was fair in the history books that the cavalry's winning was a great victory, and when the Indians won it was a massacre."

CORRECT: "We used to root for the Indians against the cavalry, because we didn't think it was fair in the history books that when the cavalry won it was a great victory, and when the Indians won it was a massacre."

Dick Gregory

Misplaced and Dangling Modifiers

People often accidentally use modifiers in such a way that it is not clear who or what is doing the doing or to whom or to what the deed is done. In such cases, the modifiers are misplaced because they are not securely attached to what they're supposed to modify. "While eating the oyster, Margot saw Irene wince." Who's eating the oyster, Margot or Irene? If it's Irene, the sentence should read "Margot saw Irene wince as she ate the oyster." Now what about, "Half-eaten, Irene sneaked the oyster onto her lap"? Obviously Irene is not half-eaten, so we fix the sentence to read, "Irene sneaked the half-eaten oyster onto her lap." Always keep modifying words and phrases as close as possible to what they modify.

INCORRECT: Hopefully, it won't rain.

CORRECT: I hope it won't rain.

It can't hope, therefore *hopefully* is incorrct in the sentence.

INCORRECT: Going home, the walk was slippery.

CORRECT: Going home, I found the walk slippery.

The *walk* didn't go home, yet *going home*, by being placed next to it, is modifying it.

INCORRECT: To think clearly, some logic is needed.

CORRECT: To think clearly, you should learn some logic.

Logic can't think clearly.

Modifiers that aren't close to what they modify cause confusion. Look at the following sentence:

John Smith hereinafter known as the party of the first part and delagatee of the estate in question as prescribed under section IV, paragraph fifteen of the state administrative code governing the transfer of estates, *is hereby delegated* the sole authority to represent said estate in court.

The main idea of the sentence is "John Smith is delegated"; everything else is a modifier. These modifiers disrupt the main idea making for difficult reading. To check for these problems, underline the main idea in each sentence. Then check the modifiers. See if you've got too many words between the subject and the verb.

PUNCTUATION

Mastery of punctuation means the ability to show without ambiguity what the parts of a written thought are and how they relate to one another. Punctuation marks the pauses and emphases the writer needs to make his or her meaning clear. Thus punctuation marks do what they can to transcribe your meaningful pauses to the printed page. In most cases you can punctuate by sound, that is, by reading your sentence aloud and hearing where the pauses occur. The punctuation mark tells the reader to slow down here, interrupt himself there, or make a full stop elsewhere.

Semicolon

The semicolon allows you to join two or three or even more related sentences so as to form a single, complex thought. But don't try to join anything less than complete sentences with it. If you can replace your semicolon with a period, your construction is acceptable, but if you can't, substitute a comma for the semicolon. It is mainly used between closely related independent clauses which balance or contrast with each other.

EXAMPLES:

Autocratic power springs from the will of the ruler; democratic power rises from the will of the people.

A beauty is a woman you notice; a charmer is one who notices you.

Note: The second example could have been written correctly in other ways; however, none is as effective as the version using the semicolon.

A beauty is a woman you notice.

A charmer is one who notices you.

A beauty is a woman you notice, while a charmer is one who notices you.

Commas

Insert a comma wherever your voice pauses when reading aloud. If that rule is too vague for you, here are more specific instances when you need to use commas.

Put commas before the coordinator—and, but, for, or, nor, yet, still—when joining independent clauses.

EXAMPLE:

Wear your jacket, or you will catch cold.

Put commas between all terms in a series, including the last two.

EXAMPLE:

I like crayfish, oysters, shrimp, and crabs.

Set off parenthetical openers and afterthoughts with a comma.

EXAMPLE:

Besides, I hate fishing.

Enclose parenthetical insertions with a pair of commas.

EXAMPLE:

The car, a 1908 Model T, is worth a quarter of a million dollars.

Use a comma between the main clause and a subordinate clause when the subordinate clause comes first.

EXAMPLE:

While the angry crowd outside the embassy waited, the ambassador met newsmen inside.

In certain coordinate constructions, a comma can replace a missing, but implied, sentence element.

EXAMPLE:

Some were punctual; others, late (*were* is implied).

Warning: Never attempt to join two independent clauses with a comma.

The new medical plan was comprehensive, the union negotiator was pleased.

You can correct this error in several ways:

The new medical plan was comprehensive; the union negotiator was pleased.

The new medical plan was comprehensive. The union negotiator was pleased.

The new medical plan was comprehensive, so the union negotiator was pleased.

Because the new medical plan was comprehensive, the union negotiator was pleased.

Parentheses

Parentheses give you a way of inserting into a sentence a piece of incidental information.

EXAMPLE:

Although the company had not expected a significant yield from the new well (they had drilled it only as an experiment), it produced a thousand barrels a day.

Dashes

The dash, like the comma and the parentheses, is a separator. Each sets off parenthetical matter. But the dash is different from the parentheses in that it should be used when the matter to be set off needs emphasis.

EXAMPLE:

To be middle-aged is to be—well, *what* is it?

H. L. Mencken

Colon

The colon joins related thoughts but only when the first thought introduces the second.

EXAMPLE:

Music is more than something mechanical: it is an expression of emotion.

The most common use of a colon is to introduce a list or series.

EXAMPLE:

The director listed the following plays: *The Crucible, Ah! Wilderness, The Playboy of the Western World,* and *Saint Joan.*

The colon is also used to introduce a quotation when it's larger than a single sentence.

Exclamation Points

Don't use exclamation points in any kind of professional writing. However, in the case of writing a speech, you must use an exclamation point after true exclamations.

EXAMPLE:

What a predicament!

Square Brackets

Use square brackets [ ] when you want to insert something you say into a quotation. Don't insert your interjection in parentheses ( ) because your reader will not know the insertion is in your words.

EXAMPLE:

"It [*The Elements of Style*] had been privately printed by the author."

Quotation Marks

Put quotation marks around quotations that "run directly into your text" (like this), but not around long quotations set off from the text and indented. Periods and commas go inside quotation marks; semicolons and colons go outside.

EXAMPLE:

Holding an August 23, 1915 article from the *Free Press,* the lawyer focused on the phrase, "Preparedness, the root of all war."

Ellipsis

Use three spaced periods ... (the ellipsis mark) when you omit something from a quotation.

EXAMPLE:

"Squint, you will ruin me. You will ruin my future. Don't have me discover you. They are sure to think I planned this. . . . [The first period indicates the sentence is finished. The next three are the ellipsis mark which indicates something has been left out of the quotation.]

I'll tell you what I'll do. Knock on some other porthole and let someone else discover you, and I'll come along and say, 'a worthy case. Something must be done about this boy.' "[3]

Henry Ford, The Wayward Capitalist

Hyphen

Hyphenate two or more words serving together as an adjective. Unhyphenated words acquire hyphens when moved to an adjectival position.

Hyphenate prefixes to proper names.
Hyphenate to avoid double i's and triple consonants.
Hyphenate two-word numbers.

EXAMPLES:

a steak-and-potatoes man	un-American
internal-combustion engines	twenty-nine operations
mass-production techniques	anti-intellectual
five-dollar wage	bell-like
war-mad world	twenty-one
anti-Semitism	

Apostrophe

An apostrophe is used with an s to form the possessive case of many nouns.

EXAMPLES:

New York City's drinking water is remarkably pure.

The waitress's uniform was soiled.

Sixteen men and one woman attended the managers' meeting.

Warning: Its is the possessive form of *it.*
        It's means *it is.*

An apostrophe is used to mark the omission of letters in a word or date.

I'll, I'm, you'll

the class of '56

Footnotes

In reports or articles, the writer often obtains information from printed sources. To show that this has been done and to lend authority to the statements, the writer must indicate his or her indebtedness in footnotes. All direct quotations must be acknowledged in the text also.

Footnotes can either appear at the end of the article or report (called endnotes) or at the bottom of the page on which quoted. There are several accepted forms for footnoting, so the writer should find out which is preferred by his or her company.

Footnotes are numbered consecutively, in the order in which the quoted, paraphrased, or summarized material occurs in the text. Footnote numbers in the text are raised slightly above the typewritten line of copy. In scientific writing, however, they are not raised but enclosed in parentheses. The footnote number in the text identifies the numbered note in which the source of information appears.

CONFUSING WORDS

It's time now to put aside general principles and get to particulars. The words that follow commonly cause confusion. You can read the list now and then refer to it later as the need arises.

affect/effect *Affect* means to produce an effect. Don't use it as a noun.

> Fear affects the mind.

As a noun, *effect* means result; as a verb, *effect* means to bring about.

> What was the effect?

> He effected a total change.

aggravate Aggravate means to add gravity to something already bad enough. It does not mean to *irritate* as in, my children aggravate me, which is an incorrect use of *aggravate*.

> The damp house aggravated my flu. (Correct)

all right *All right* is right; *alright* is wrong.

all together/altogether *All together* means all members of a group gathered together; *altogether* is an adverb meaning wholly or completely.

> At last, we're all together for Christmas.

> The scene from the deck was altogether breathtaking.

allusion/illusion Although the two words are often pronounced similarly, don't confuse them. *Allusion* means an indirect reference or a casual reference to something and is followed by *to*. *Illusion* means an unreal image or a false impression and is followed by *of*.

> They made allusions to his personal life.

> Everyone outgrows his illusions of grandeur.

among/between When speaking of just two persons or things, use *between*; of three or more, use *among*.

already/all ready These two are not synonymous. *Already* is an adverb meaning prior to a specified time; *all ready* means completely prepared.

> The signs of spring were already in evidence.
>
> The group was all ready to leave.

can/may *Can* means able. It should not be used as a substitute for *may*.

> Can I go downtown?
>
> Yes, you are able to go downtown, but no, you may not go.

criterion/criteria *Criterion* is the singular form; *criteria*, the plural.

> A single criterion has been established.
>
> The criteria for entrance are stiff.
>
> Allied words: medium, media
>
> > memorandum, memoranda
> >
> > datum, data
> >
> > stratum, strata

disinterested/uninterested If you are *disinterested*, you are unbiased or impartial. If you are *uninterested*, you are not interested.

> Please find a disinterested person to settle the dispute.
>
> The crowd is obviously uninterested in our dispute.

famous/infamous If a person is well known and acclaimed, that person is *famous*. But if a person is known because of being disreputable, that person is *infamous*.

farther/further *Farther* is preferred to express greater distance in space. *Further* is restricted to a sense of greater advancement in time or degree.

> New Orleans is farther from New York than Pittsburgh is.
>
> I am further along in graduate school than my brother is.

however Avoid starting a sentence with *however* when the meaning is *nevertheless*. The word is better when it is not the first word in the sentence.

> No: The road was almost washed out. However, we at last succeeded in getting to Reef House.
>
> Yes: The road was almost washed out. At last, however, we succeeded in getting to Reef House.

When *however* comes first, it means *to whatever extent* or *in whatever way.*

> However you advise him, he will do as he pleases anyway.

imply/infer   If a writer has *implied* something, he or she has hinted it or insinuated it instead of saying it outright; if the reader gets the hint, he *inferred* it, that is, deduced the veiled point.

> Skiing implies athletic ability.

> Since he was a skier, I inferred that he was athletic.

irregardless   There is no such word as *irregardless.* Use *regardless.*

its/it's   *Its* is the possessive form of *it. It's* is a contraction of *it is.* The confusion occurs because normally possession is indicated by the apostrophe. In the case of *its,* there is a special rule. *Its* belongs to a class of words called prenominal or pure possessives. Others are: *hers, theirs, yours, ours.*

-ize   Don't coin verbs by adding this suffix. Some verbs do end in *ize:* summarize, temporize, fraternize, harmonize, fertilize. But words like *containerize, customize, prioritize, finalize,* are simply nouns to which people have attached *ize* in order to create a verb. These are jargon words, and should be avoided.

lay   *Lay* is a transitive verb which means it needs an object.

> The hen lays eggs.

> I lay the book on the table.

> I lie down.

lend/loan   *Lend* is a verb; *loan* is a noun.

> I will lend you $100 since you need the loan badly.

like   Do not use as a conjunction; it is a preposition. *Like,* then, governs nouns, pronouns, and phrases. Clauses use *as.*
Remember the old slogan, "Winston tastes good like a cigarette should"? Millions complained because it was bad English. It should have been, "Winston tastes good as a cigarette should." The company loved the controversy, and later amended its copy to look like this:

> *as*
> "Winston tastes good ~~like~~ a cigarette should."

> EXAMPLE:

> She swims like a fish.

nauseous/nauseated   *Nauseous* means sickening to contemplate; *nauseated* means sick to your stomach. So don't say "I feel nauseous" unless you mean you have that effect on others.

none   *None* means *no one* and therefore takes a singular verb.

> None of them is perfect.

Other words which take singular verbs:
each, every, everyone, nobody.

only   Make sure you put *only* immediately before the word it actually modifies.

> Sam only plays golf on weekends.
>
> Sam plays golf only on weekends.

The first sentence says that Sam plays golf on weekends to the exclusion of everything else. The second sentence implies that the only time Sam plays golf is on weekends. Which do you mean? Be careful about placing *only*.

precede   *Precede* means to come before. Don't confuse the word with *proceed* which means to go forward.

> The army proceeded to attack the enemy.
>
> The maid of honor preceded the bride down the aisle.

principal/principle   *Principal* means chief and can be used as a noun (principal of the school) or as an adjective (the principal witness). *Principle* means a rule or a basic truth and can only be used as a noun.

> Be true to your principles.

real   Do not use *real* for *very*. *Real* is an adjective and an adjective may not modify an adverb or another adjective. So "it was real good" is bad English. Write instead:

> It was very good.
>
> It was really good.

secondly, thirdly   Never use these. If you do, you should have used *firstly*, and there's no such word as *firstly*. So stick to *first, second, third,* and so on.

thusly   *Thus* is an adverb. To add the suffix -ly is redundant.

type   *Type* is not a synonym for *kind of*.

WRONG:	RIGHT:
that type employee	that kind of employee
small, home-type inns	small, homelike inns
a new type engine	an engine of a new design

unique   *Unique* means only one of its kind. There can be no degrees of uniqueness. So you can't say *rather unique* or *most unique* or *very unique*.

-wise This pseudo-suffix should be avoided. It is so overused it's become a cliché. How often do you hear words like taxwise, pricewise, marriagewise?

Notes

1. Michael Adelstein, *Contemporary Business Writing*. New York: Random House, 1971, p. 178.
2. Theodore Bernstein, *Miss Thistlebottom's Hobgoblins*. New York: Farrar, Straus & Giroux, 1971, p. 174.
3. Carol Gelderman, *Henry Ford, the Wayward Capitalist*. New York: The Dial Press, 1981, p. 115.

CHAPTER *6*

Editing

This chapter is like the quality-control stage at the end of an assembly line. Use it first to identify your errors and then correct them. Don't begin to revise the moment you finish writing. You have a much better chance of putting yourself in the reader's place if you get away from the writing for a while and come back fresh.

REVISION

All good writing is self-taught. An instructor or a book can help, but you must learn to spot your own errors and work out your own ways of removing them. Every writer revises. Please don't think that I sat down one day and beginning with the first word in the preface wrote straight on to the last word of the epilogue. I have rewritten the entire manuscript twice and some parts of it a half-dozen times.

Interviewer:	How much rewriting do you do?
Hemingway:	It depends. I rewrote the ending of *Farewell to Arms*, the last page of it, thirty-nine times before I was satisfied.
Interviewer:	Was there some technical problem there? What was it that had stumped you?
Hemingway:	Getting the words right.

> I have never thought of myself as a good writer. Anyone who wants reassurance of that should read one of my first drafts. But I'm one of the world's great rewriters.
>
> James Michener

In 1940 when England was threatened with invasion, the government, determined that the disaster of France should not be repeated, was anxious that panic-stricken civilians should not clog the roads (as they had done in France) and impede the military.

A slogan, "Stay Put" was coined. At somebody's suggestion (probably Winston Churchill) this was changed to "Stand Firm." "Stay Put" has the air of a contemptuous command to inferiors. "Stand Firm"is the adulation to heroes from heroes.

Locke in his essay "Of Civil Government" wrote: "Civil interests I call life, liberty, health, and indolency of body; and the possession of outward things, such as money, lands, houses, furniture, and the like."

Jefferson, following Locke, wrote: "Life, liberty, and the pursuit of happiness."

There are seven known versions of Lincoln's Gettysburg Address. The phrase, "It is altogether fitting and proper that we should do this" was originally written as, "This we may, in all propriety, do."

Rarely does anyone dash off a first draft and call it a finished paper. Samuel Johnson said, "What is written without effort is in general read without pleasure." That's true enough, but he could have added "or without profit." If you want to do well in your job, you've got to write exceptionally. To write exceptionally, you'll have to work hard at revising.

The following, a final draft as compared with a first draft of a 600-word paper on national health insurance, is an example of the improvement good revisions can make.

	Final Draft	**First Draft**
There is no announcement of the thesis in the first paragraph of the first draft as there is in the final. The first sentence in first draft contains a faulty parallelism; this is corrected in the final.	The richest nation on earth has a health care system that provides the wealthy and insured with too much medicine, the poor and underprivileged with too little, enjoys more expertise and facilities on its East coast than on its West, permits rises in cost 20% to 30% faster than the consumer	The richest nation on earth has a health care system that provides the wealthy and insured with too much medicine, ignores the poor and underprivileged, has more expertise and facilities in the east than the west, boasts an infant mortality rate twice that of Sweden's and rises in cost 20%

price index, and acknowledges an infant mortality rate twice that of Sweden. The disparity by class and region which characterizes the American health care system belies the Constitution's promise of equality for all. The best possible medical care should be a right of every citizen. A comprehensive National Health Insurance Plan is one way to make sure that each American can claim his or her health-care franchise.

An across-the-board insurance plan in which the government collects money from a payroll tax and uses this money to pay every American for his health needs by reimbursing doctors and hospitals for their services is the simplest method of ensuring health-care for all because it uses the system already in structure. France and Germany have such plans which work well. By contrast, England has a direct provision system of health-care where the government owns the hospitals, purchases all equipment, and hires personnel. By eliminating a supply-and-demand situation, the English government created problems. Anyone with an emergency is treated fairly promptly, but pity the poor hernia sufferer who might have to wait two years for surgical relief. The insurance plan, then, as developed in France and Germany, is a workable national health strategy.

In the first draft the quote from Kennedy is vague, so the writer wisely got rid of it in the final. Why switch tone by introducing first person in a paper which tries to be professorial as the writer does in first draft? Wisely, in final draft he writes it all in third person. What are "defined poor people"? The writer realized how silly the expression was and excised it. The second paragraph in the first draft is too long. Note transition from last sentence in first paragraph of final draft to first sentence in the second paragraph. In the final draft the second paragraph sticks to its topic, announced in first sentence, government insurance plans. The second paragraph in first draft jumps all over the place.

to 30% faster than the consumer price index. The nation we are talking about is the United States where the constitution states equality for all and where disparity by class and region punctuates the health care system.

Many people feel the best possible medical care should be a "right" of all citizens; one such person is Senator Edward Kennedy: "I believe good health care should be a right of all Americans. Health is so basic to man's abilities to bring to fruition his opportunities as an American that each of us should guarantee the best possible health care to every American at a cost he can afford. Health care is not a luxury or an optional choice we can do without." I share the senator's views and fully endorse the idea of a comprehensive National Health Insurance Plan. The justifications of such are simple; just access to proper care would be greatly improved. Presently 20 percent of defined poor people in this nation are not eligible for any sort of Medicare or Medicaid, providing an insurmountable hurdle for many who dream of a better life. Secondly, financial hardship caused by catastrophic illness could be dramatically reduced or eliminated. It is a fact that most families today cannot financially endure a grave or prolonged illness within their household, even with insurance coverage. This constitutes a national disgrace when the mean family income is now close to $20,000 per year. Thirdly, a National Health

The third paragraph of the final draft sticks to its announced topic, an American health insurance plan. By contrast, third paragraph of first draft contains a topic which has been partially discussed in the second paragraph.

Everyone recognizes current inequities in the American health-care system, so why not eradicate this unfairness by federal legislation? A National Health Insurance Plan would embrace those persons presently ineligible for medicare and medicaid (20 percent of all Americans below the poverty level), and it would eliminate financial hardship, and in many cases disaster, caused by catastrophic illness which strikes millions of Americans. Most families, even with private insurance coverage, cannot endure prolonged illness. This is a disgrace considering the mean family income in the United States is close to $20,000. Finally, national health insurance would furnish central control for the present chaotic system of health-care delivery. This central control, in turn, could be used to lower cost. The federal government, for example, which would pay out all claims, could mandate 100 percent reimbursement for minor surgery which is performed in a doctor's office while only paying 50 percent of the fee for the same surgery done in a hospital. Moreover, the government could initiate uniform reimbursement codes for doctors and hospitals; currently various government agencies and private companies set fluctuating scales of payment.

Since the need for a national insurance plan is so obvious, and since good health care is every American's birthright, the plan this country adopts should cover every citizen. Because Social Security, Assistance to

Insurance Plan would give central control to a chaotic system. With costs being paid by the federal government across-the-board incentives could be initiated aimed at lowering hospital costs. One example would be 100 percent reimbursement for minor surgical procedures done in a doctor's office with only a 50 percent reimbursement given when the patient elects to have the procedure done in the hospital. Further the government could initiate uniform prospective reimbursement codes where doctors would only receive so much for a particular operation and hospitals could only receive so much for their rooms. All these things are only partially possible today with so many government agencies and private companies setting their own guidelines for the correct disbursement of insurance benefits.

Many Americans fear government getting involved in medical care further because they have seen the federal government's ability to waste funds. This is why the insurance plan should be across the board, covering all Americans. Today much money is spent in the Social Security program, Assistance to Families of Dependent Children, Food Stamps, and Medicare and Medicaid just determining eligibility. With all Americans eligible no such problem would exist.

Many persons opposed to National Health Insurance point out the problems of Great Britain's system. In the U. K. one

The fourth paragraph of the final draft also sticks to its announced topic, eligibility. The fourth paragraph of the first draft is badly out of place. The placement of this information in the final draft is better.

The fifth paragraph of the first draft is really just a sentence hanging there, belonging to nothing. The last paragraph of the first draft is the only one that is correctly placed.

Families with Dependent Children, the Food Stamp programs, and Medicare and Medicaid set eligibility standards, a great deal of money and effort are expended in enforcing these rules. An across-the-board plan will eliminate all eligibility tests.

No one denies that national health insurance will be expensive. But health care should not be a marketable commodity. People cannot and should not put a price on the abatement of human suffering. The pursuit of happiness is not possible when one is sick and unable to afford relief. Quite simply, good medical attention should be a right as much as voting is a right. Strong legislation to make good health-care every American's right is long overdue.

can wait up to two years for elective surgery. This is because they have a direct provision system whereby the government controls every aspect of health care from hiring medical personnel to building new facilities. This is why the United States should go the insurance route when developing a national health strategy. France and Germany have enjoyed great success with national insurance plans.

With everyone insured, let's say through a payroll tax, the existing medical system would remain intact but government would have the opportunity to get a bid on costs.

I suppose the best argument for National Health Insurance amid the cries of "socialism" is to say health care is not a marketable commodity. People cannot and should not attempt to put a price on the abatement of human suffering. The pursuit of happiness is not possible when one is sick and unable to afford relief. Quite simply medicine is a right as much as it is a right to vote in this country. Strong legislation to protect this right is long overdue.

The basic problem with the first draft was organization. One wonders if the writer prepared adequately. Whether he did or didn't spend enough time prewriting is not relevant to his revisions which saved the day. Of course if he had done adequate preparation, he would not have had to revise so extensively. If you look back to Chapter 1 at the money market fund article, you'll see that there was little revising to do (only one paragraph was out of place) chiefly because the writer expended effort in preparation. No matter how much time you spend in getting ready to write your first draft, you will surely have to do some revising. The following checklists will help you do this efficiently.

CHECKLISTS

After you gain confidence in your ability to write clear papers, you will not need to spend much time with the following checklists, but until you do feel completely confident, answer each question honestly.

Checklist for Articles and Speeches

Do you have a clear-cut, well-defined point of view about a manageable topic? _____

Is that point of view forcefully and unambiguously stated in one sentence (usually at the end of the introductory paragraph)? _____

Does your organizing idea control your approach to the subject; that is, do you stick to your point? _____

Is your article or speech unified? _____

Do you avoid unsupported generalities? _____

Do you have forceful examples? _____

Is your evidence suited to your purpose? _____

Is your paper coherent? _____

Does it have a strong sense of direction or does it wander haphazardly from one unrelated point to another? _____

Does your organizing idea dictate your organization? _____

Does the order in which you develop your points seem to follow inevitably from your organizing idea? _____

Do you have a topic sentence in each paragraph? _____

In your topic sentence, do you promise all that you will discuss, and then discuss nothing that you have not promised? _____

Have you underlined the organizing idea from the first paragraph and the topic sentence from each subsequent paragraph? Do these provide an outline for your paper? _____

Do you have a definitive conclusion that reasserts your organizing idea? _____

Does your tone suit your purpose? _____

Is it too lighthearted, too solemn, too personal, too impersonal, too casual, too stilted, too impassioned, too diffident? _____

Did you consider your topic and your audience, and let the occasion dictate your tone? _____

Is your vocabulary concrete? _____

Have you avoided clichés? _____

Do you avoid the passive voice? _____

Is every sentence a real sentence, containing a subject and a verb and presenting a complete idea? _____

Is every sentence one sentence only, not two that are incorrectly combined by a comma? _____

Have you inserted commas whenever the rules and your sense of the sentence demand? _____

Have you deleted unnecessary commas? _____

Have you remembered to insert all necessary apostrophes, both for contraction and possession? _____

Have you used quotation marks properly on all quotations? _____

Have you used colons and parentheses, if at all, sparingly and correctly? _____

Do your questions end in question marks? _____

Checklist for Reports

Should your report have a cover page? _____

Is your title short and descriptive? _____

Is your report accurately dated? _____

Have you proofread your report remembering to check your arithmetic? _____

Do you need a letter of transmittal? _____

Do you need a table of contents? _____

Have you covered: purpose, _____

                  conclusions, _____

                  recommendations? _____

Are your readers familiar with all past events or reports which may have a bearing on this report? _____

What is the purpose of your report? _____

Have you given an adequate description of how the investigation was conducted? _____

Are the scope and limitations of the report clearly defined? _____

Is the report clear? _____

Is the report concise? _____

Is the report readable? _____

Do your paragraphs have a topic sentence? _____

Is there more than one topic in any one paragraph?   _____

Are your words simple?   _____

Are your words concrete?   _____

Have you used unnecessary words?   _____

Have you used active verbs?   _____

Is your writing conversational?   _____

Have you checked for typographical errors?   _____

Have you eliminated clichés?   _____

Should you have used tables or graphs?   _____

Does your report clearly indicate a course of action?   _____

Does your reader have any unanswered questions?   _____

After you've done all the revising and checking you feel is necessary, see if you can't find someone to read it over and make comments. You can encourage your appointed editor by quoting from George Bernard Shaw who often sent early drafts of his plays to his friend Ellen Terry, the actress, for criticism. Once she said she feared to suggest changes on his manuscript. He wrote back:

> Oh, bother the MSS., mark them as much as you like: what else are they for? Mark everything that strikes you. I may consider a thing 49 times; but if you consider it, it will be considered 50 times; and a line 50 times considered is 2 percent better than a line 49 times considered. And it is the final 2 percent that makes the difference between excellence and mediocrity.

TIGHTENING

Benjamin Franklin, who helped Thomas Jefferson write the Declaration of Independence, a skillfully revised document, once told this anecdote to Mr. Jefferson:

> When I was a journeyman printer, one of my companions, an apprentice Hatter, having served out his time, was about to open a shop for himself. His first concern was to have a handsome signboard, with a proper inscription. He composed it in these words: "John Thompson, Hatter,

makes and sells hats for ready money" with a figure of a hat subjoined. But he thought he would submit it to his friends for their amendments. The first he shewed it to thought the word "hatter" tautologous, because followed by the words "makes hats" which shew he was a hatter. It was struck out. The next observed that the word "makes" might as well be omitted, because his customers would not care who made the hats. If good and to their mind, they would buy, by whomsoever made. He struck it out. A third said he thought the words "for ready money" were useless as it was not the custom of the place to sell on credit. Every one who purchased expected to pay. They were parted with, and the inscription now stood "John Thompson sells hats." "*Sells* hats" says his next friend? Why nobody will expect you to give them away. What then is the use of that word? It was stricken out and "hats" followed it, the rather, as there was one painted on the board. So his inscription was reduced ultimately to "John Thompson" with the figure of a hat subjoined.[1]

Principle: Don't repeat words or ideas unless they strengthen what you want to say. When you tighten what you write, you get rid of wordiness.

Consider the following wordy definition of wordiness.

Wordiness is a word that is often used by many people to express the idea that something that was written by someone in a larger number of words could have been expressed in a smaller number of words.

How much better if the writer had said, "Wordiness means using too many words."

Note

1. Ken Macrorie, *Telling Writing*. New York: Hayden Book Company, Inc., 1970, pp. 25–26.

EPILOGUE

The cover story for the May 4, 1981, *Time Magazine*, entitled, "The Money Chase. What Business Schools Are Doing to Us," claimed that training in the nation's business schools may be a cause of a current malaise in business management. A principal criticism of business schools was put best by Reginald H. Jones, a Wharton M.B.A., who had just retired as chairman of General Electric: "I think the top business schools do a good job, though they could do better at teaching communication skills and providing greater exposure to the humanities...." "If I could choose one degree for the people I hire, it would be English," a senior vice-president of the First Atlanta Corporation was quoted in the same article as saying. "I want people who can read and speak in the language we're dealing with. You can teach a group of Cub Scouts to do portfolio analysis."

So I end where I began—every professional must be a good communicator. Writing is the most complex form of communication.

APPENDIX ONE: PARTS OF SPEECH

Nouns   Nouns name something. A proper noun names a particular person, place, or thing. A common noun names a general class of things.

> EXAMPLES:
> stone, tree, house, George, America, California, committee, herd, navy

Pronouns   Pronouns stand for nouns. The noun a pronoun represents is called its antecedent.

> EXAMPLES:
> I, you, he, she, it, we, they, you, who, which, that, what, this, these, those, such, one, any, each, few, some, anyone, everyone, somebody, each, another

Verbs   Verbs express actions or state of being.

> EXAMPLES:
> hit, run, walk, meditate, is, are, sing

Adjectives   Adjectives describe nouns or pronouns

> EXAMPLES:
> green, beautiful, fat

Adverbs   Adverbs describe verbs, adjectives, or other adverbs.

> EXAMPLES:
> slightly, after

Prepositions   Prepositions link nouns or pronouns to another word in the sentence.

> EXAMPLES:
> by, from, for

Conjunctions   Conjunctions join words, phrases, and clauses.

> EXAMPLES:
> and, but, or, yet, since, because

Interjections   Interjections interrupt the usual flow of the sentence to emphasize feelings.

> EXAMPLES:
> oh, ouch, alas

APPENDIX TWO: READABILITY FORMULAS

Readability formulas are procedures for computing the easy readability of a text on the basis of some of its elements: number of words per sentence, number of syllables per word, number of words on a special list. Texts with short words and sentences come out best on readability tests.

Rudolf Flesch (Flesch Formula) and Robert Gunning (Gunning Fog Index) are two of the best known formulators of readability formulas. Douglas Mueller, president of Gunning-Mueller Writing Institute in Santa Barbara, California, carries on the work of the late Robert Gunning, who invented the Fog Index, a way to compute the years of schooling needed to understand a piece of writing. The idea is to achieve a low Fog Index since people prefer to read well below their educational level.

To give you an idea of what your Fog Index should or could be, consider the following:

TV Guide—Fog Index of 6
Wall Street Journal—Fog Index of 11
Time—Fog Index of 11
Newsweek—Fog Index of 11

Because Flesch, Gunning, and their imitators have been extolling the virtues of their readability formulas for four decades, and because

Here's how to compute your own Fog Index:

1. Find the average number of words per sentence in a sample of your writing 100 to 200 words long. Treat clearly independent clauses as separate sentences. Example: Caesar came; he saw; he conquered. This counts as three sentences.

2. Calculate the percentage of words having three or more syllables. Don't count capitalized words, easy combinations like "pawnbroker," or verbs that reach three syllables by addition of *-es* or *-ed*.

3. Add the average sentence length to the percentage of big words and multiply the total by 0.4. The resulting number is the years of schooling needed to understand what you've written. If the piece of writing you are analyzing is lengthy, take other samples at random, repeat the process, and average the results.

the formulas meet a genuine need for convenient and inexpensive ways to estimate the difficulty of written prose, readability formulas have been widely adopted. I think they are overrated.

Readability formulas do not ensure comprehensibility. They do not detect misused words, ungrammatical sentences, illogical prepositions, or nonsense. The formulas do not measure organization, effectiveness, or relevance to the audience. The formulas simply tap a few of the superficial characteristics of a text that may contribute to complexity—long words and long sentences.

Recently a readability formula was applied to Erskine Caldwell's *Georgia Boy* and James Joyce's *Finnegan's Wake*. Both got the same readability score, yet *Georgia Boy* is a novel easily accessible to the average reader while *Finnegan's Wake* is the most difficult-to-understand novel written in English.

Writing is too complex an activity to submit to such a simple measure as syllable and word count. Yet there is some correlation between sentence length and reading difficulty. You should neither ignore this relationship nor submit to it blindly.

INDEX